D0660813

DON'T
DIE

© 2012 Arsen S. Marsoobian.

Soob Enterprises LLC
1247 E. Foxhill DR. # 138
Fresno, CA. 93720

Cover art: Ashlee Goodwin, *City at Sunset*, 2012
Book design by Hive Creative.

PAPASOOB.COM

Some content from Bronnie Ware is used with permission from http://inspirationandchai.com/ Regrets-of-the-Dying.html. Bronnie Ware is a writer and songwriter from Australia who spent several years caring for dying people. Based on this article, Bronnie has now released a full length book, THE TOP FIVE REGRETS OF THE DYING - A Life Transformed by the Dearly Departing. It is a memoir of her own life and how it was transformed through the regrets of the dying people she cared for. For more information, please visit www.bronnieware.com.

DON'T DIE

3 Essential Truths FOR YOUR Fulfilled and Happy Life (regardless of your age)

ARSEN S. MARSOOBIAN

This book is dedicated to
my children and grandchildren
who I pray will one day, read and apply
the truths in this book and have a
fulfilled and happy life.

My oldest son, Brad Marsoobian
and his wife Pam Kendrick.
My daughter Lori Marsoobian Thomas,
Bryan Marsoobian (the original SOOB)
and his wife Julie Kershaw.

To the ones who keep me young and give
me reason to keep on living, my grandchildren.
Taylor Marsoobian, Morgan Marsoobian,
Nicholas Marsoobian, Sydney Marsoobian,
Renny Thomas, and Matthew Marsoobian.

Love you all.

CONTENTS

PART TWO: THE UNIVERSAL TRUTH OF BODY

PART THREE: THE UNIVERSAL TRUTH OF SOUL

THE BONUS

ACKNOWLEDGEMENTS

I would like to acknowledge and thank all the people that have helped me along the way in bringing this book to you. The book in its current form would not have been produced without each of their input and support.

Lynn Rose, author, speaker, entertainer, and friend who has encouraged and supported me the last four years to reach this position in my life.

Les Brown, world-renowned speaker, best-selling author, and friend whose prompting and support got me off the couch and back in the game of life at age 74.

Mark Victor Hansen, author of *Chicken Soup For The Soul* and international speaker whose "Wealth, Wisdom, Writers Program" gave me the foundation and encouragement I needed to write.

Michelle Prince, author of *Winning In Life Now* and national speaker who gave me an outline and accountability to write this book when I didn't think it was worth writing.

Tom Sommers CLU, my spiritual father and Executive Director of the Fresno Christian Business Men's Connection who was willing to edit the spelling and grammar in the very early stages of the manuscript.

Jack Hanna, "Cowboy Jack," California high school teacher, baseball coach, head of the 'Sons of the San Joaquin' music group, television personality, and friend who tirelessly assisted with spelling and grammar correction in the very early stages of this manuscript.

Richard Smith, author of *God Versus The Rest of US*, Associate Pastor, and general manager for a large warehouse distribution company, who made me believe that I have something to offer the world, and edited and provided constant feedback as this book developed.

Rosellen Kershaw, friend and inlaw, philanthropist, political activist, woman who has made a tremendous impact on the community of Fresno, and recipient of many awards, who, at age 89, reads 5 or more books a week and read several drafts of this book making valuable suggestions.

Special thanks to my friend and writing partner, Leslie Lindeman, without whose contribution this book would not be all that it is.

Thank You All.

PAPA SOOB

PREFACE

Let me ask you a couple questions straight from the heart. Are you living your life full on? In the morning when you first realize you are awake, does your heart beat a little faster because you are excited for a new day?

For most of my life, I would have answered these questions with, "Not really," and, "No way." But then a couple things happened. First, thanks to a series of heart attacks—yes, you got that right, I said, "Thanks," because I'm grateful for what I learned from them… So thanks to a couple heart attacks, and thanks to the work I've been doing my entire life to understand how I can best achieve the things I want, I am in a different and better place than I have ever been.

That's why it was time for me to write this book—to round up what I've learned and to share it with people I know can benefit from it. You're reading these words now and I'll bet that means this book is for you.

It's not easy to live a "full-on" life. We have needs, or perceived needs, that seem to push in the direction of the dreary and the mundane. But it doesn't have to be that way. In fact, I believe it's not supposed to be that way!

Now I want to tell you something about myself that many authors would consider information it's not best to share. I'm 77 years old. We live in a culture in which once you hit 40 or 50, your relevance starts to fade. It's time for Botox, a face lift, liposuction, a sports car and whatever kind of makeover you can think of and afford.

Don't go down that road. I can tell you there is no satisfaction to be had down there.

I've chased youth, I've chased money, I've chased romance, and I've won and lost them all. More than once.

But I've never achieved satisfaction through any of those things that can in any way compare to the experiences I have gained and the fulfillment I have experienced by pursuing the inner happiness and joy I describe in these pages.

I think you have a sense of what I am talking about. I think you are on to it too. And I think this book will take you what I'm guessing is the relatively short distance from where you are to a better place you absolutely want to be. And where you deserve to be too.

You're not the first to read these pages. I didn't publish this book until I had run it past people I trust to tell me the truth. It made a difference for them and that's why I believe it will for you too.

As a 77 year-old I can say to you with a robust confidence and all the love in my heart (which has escaped the grave and been repaired many times over), "Don't wait!" It doesn't get better. It doesn't get easier. Information, inspiration, a few key changes and some diligent practice are the key to achieving, having and enjoying the things you want in your life. All you will get from reading and working on the exercises at the end of this book, is everything your heart desires.

Thank you for taking a part of this amazing journey with me. I appreciate you, I trust you, I believe in the goodness inside you and in the contribution I know you make to our world.

God bless you.
Arsen

INTRODUCTION

They sent me home from the hospital on December 31, 1999. I felt like a newborn baby, completely helpless, having just arrived in the world after a long, strange, traumatic journey, and I had whatever there was of my unpredictable, unknowable life waiting in front of me. It might be a day. It might be a decade. I didn't know.

I wasn't a baby at all. I was 65 years old and I had dodged a pretty high mortality rate for quadruple bypass surgery at the time. That said, I had been having thoughts about throwing in the towel. I could have gone to the hospital to die, and maybe I did. But something happened there, besides a doctor and a fleet of nurses doing an amazing job of not letting me go.

Late one night, when I was alone in my hospital room, I remember seeing people beckoning to me. Some wanted me to come with them to a very dark place. Others were surrounded by crosses and they gave off a beautiful feeling.

I am not what you would call a New Age man. I was born during the Depression. I've had a couple careers, one as a life insurance salesman and one in government. I don't eat tofu or do yoga.

So when I tell you there were people beckoning to me, you can know I'm being straight with you. I would direct you also to a ton of literature about people who have gone through similar experiences and seen and experienced similar things. Some times they are called, "near-death experiences." I don't think I died, but I can tell you I was on the doorstep. I could have died.

What surprised me was it felt like a choice, like ordering steak off a menu. I will come back to this story in more detail later in the book. For now, know that many people would say I should have died. I was certainly programmed for it. There are a lot of statistics that point to the mortality of men the same age I was then, who are recently retired and not sure what's next for them. I was in that zone, a zone that people of my generation pass through, most of them men and for a lot of them it's the final passage of their lives. But I wasn't ready. I don't know where it came from, but I still had a taste for life, and in a strange way, I was suddenly hungrier than ever.

Have you ever noticed that a lot of people die within months of retirement? The national average for life after retirement today is 5 years and 7 months. Years ago when I was in my thirties, I started to be aware of this problem. A person would have a big retirement party announcement in the paper and in six months to a year they were back in the paper—in the obituary section.

Then I found out that the retirement age was set at 65 because people in America weren't living much past age 64 or 68. What was happening, I used to wonder?

Maybe it was because I worked in the insurance industry where actuarial tables are key to what we do, but I began to think about death and about life. How could I live longer? I was getting close to the question that would really change my life; it's a cousin of the "live longer" question. The improved question is, "How do I live better?" Not, how do I bring more years to my life, rather, how do I bring more life to my years?

Then one day I heard a quote from comedian George Burns. He was in his mid 90s and going strong. He always had young women around him, smoking cigars, laughing and having good time. A reporter asked, "Mr. Burns, what is the secret to a long life?" George, slowly taking the cigar out of his mouth, looked closely at the reporter and answered, "Don't Die." Then he placed the cigar back in his mouth and everyone laughed. The interview was over.

For some reason I never forgot that. Was there a deeper meaning to this profound and funny line?

Then my time came. I was forced into my first retirement at age 64. I was let go by a large life insurance company I was working for at the time. Within 18 months I had two bypass surgeries right on top of each other, just 70 days apart.

The second one occurred on my 65th birthday. It was through the grace of GOD that I survived a 13-hour operation, and four days in intensive care. I was supposed to be a statistic. But I DID NOT DIE. I am alive at age 77, writing a book and living my dream.

When I came home from the hospital on December 31, 1999, I celebrated the new millennium the only way I could. I watched it happen on TV, beginning in Australia and wrapping its way all around the globe, to Europe, New York, the rest of the U.S., and finally California. I was thrilled to see it. I was happy for everyone. By the time it was the year 2000 on the West Coast, I couldn't wait to recuperate so I could get out of bed and get going. I didn't know what I was going to do, but I wanted to do it.

Let me tell you about a story I heard from Dr. Anthony Campolo, professor of sociology at Southwestern University in Philadelphia. Campolo is a platform speaker, Baptist preacher, and a very funny guy. Dr. Campolo, had his students do a survey of 50 people over the age of 95, with the question: "If you had your life to live over what would you do differently?" As you can imagine there were a lot of answers, but three things stood out and were mentioned by all of the people interviewed:

1. THEY WOULD TAKE MORE RISKS IN LIFE. (DOING)

2. THEY WOULD REFLECT MORE, BE IN THE MOMENT. (LEARNING)

3. THEY WOULD DO MORE THINGS THAT WOULD LIVE ON IN THE LIVES OF OTHERS AFTER THEY WERE GONE. (GIVING)

It was during this time that I came to understand what George Burns meant when he said, "DON'T DIE." It sounded glib and funny and he wasn't taken seriously at the time he said it. But I began to think about it, and to see the deeper meaning in it. The opposite of dying is living. But not just breathing and taking up space, rather, really treasuring my life and living as if every moment of my time on Earth makes a difference. I didn't want to just stay alive for a lot of years, I wanted to really be alive while I was living. I felt like I could do more than just not be dead. I felt like I could add more life to my years. I felt like I could make every period of my life, "The Time of My Life."

The great playwright, William Saroyan, wrote the Pulitzer Prize-winning play by this title, and in the prelude to the play he wrote this:

> In the time of your life, live—so that in that good time there shall be no ugliness or death for yourself or for any life your life touches.
>
> Seek goodness everywhere, and when it is found, bring it out of its hiding place and let it be free and unashamed. Place in matter and flesh the

least of the values, for these are the things that hold death and must pass away.

Discover in all things that which shines and is beyond corruption. Encourage virtue in whatever heart it may have been driven into secrecy and sorrow by the shame and terror of the world.

Ignore the obvious, for it is unworthy of the clear eye and kindly heart.

Be the inferior of no man, nor of any man be the superior. Remember that every man is a variation of yourself. No man's guilt is not yours, nor is any man's innocence a thing apart. Despise evil and ungodliness, but not men of ungodliness or evil.

These understand. Have no shame in being kindly and gentile, but if the time comes in the time of your life to kill, kill and have no regret. In the time of your life, live—so that in that wondrous time you shall not add to the misery and sorrow of the world, but shall smile to the infinite delight and mystery of it.

It is my prayer that as you journey through these pages, you will enjoy the stories, and that the concepts will inspire you to discover, The Time of Your Life—IS NOW. Live it full out till the end. It's never too late.

PART ONE: THE UNIVERSAL TRUTH OF MIND

CHAPTER 1
THE LEARNING PROCESS

The power to think as you wish
is the only power over which you
have absolute control.
—NAPOLEAN HILL

The baby is always the most interesting person in the elevator. I once learned, if you want to be interesting, be interested. Everyone else in the elevator is looking at the tops of their shoes or watching the lights—6 —7—8—9. But the baby is looking everywhere, she is fascinated, and she's the only one smiling. The baby is the only one in the elevator who will look you in the eye.

All these great things about the baby, are because the baby is the only one in the elevator who is learning.

There is an adage that goes, "Learn one thing every day." I am so happy you are reading this book. It tells me you want to learn. You're not done. Not by a long shot. And I don't care how old you are. You know what I'm talking about. At any age we face the temptation to put it on auto-pilot, switch on the cruise control and let the tides of life have their way with us. Before you know it, there went a decade. We're asleep. Learning is the antidote to that.

One of my favorite expressions is, "What's the take-home?" What am I learning right now that I will take home tonight and remember, and be better because of it? There is a line from a song I like by John Prine called, Angel From Montgomery. It goes:

How can a person
Go to work in the morning
Come home in the evening
And have nothing to say?

That speaks to me about making every day count, and about living my life with meaning, which are both important values to me.

There are all different kinds of theories about learning. Does learning come from our parents? Or does it come from our environment? Does it come from what we picked up in school, from our friends or from random events that may have happened to us? Or does it come from choices we make about how we want to shape our character?

My theory is, yes. It's all of that and more. From the time we are born we start to learn. Does it matter how? Not really. I'll leave that for the professors. It's enough for me to know that learning comes wherever and whenever I can find it. Another song: "You can get shown the light in the strangest of places, if you look at it right."

Have I learned from Shakespeare? Sure. "To thine own self be true." I'm not George Clooney. I'm not Hussein Bolt. I'm me, and I'm going to be the best me I can be. Oscar Wilde said, "Be yourself, everyone else is already taken."

But I've also learned from watching a bunch of ants on my patio. Look at them moving something thousands of times their weight. How can they do that? Cooperation! Determination! Holy smokes, imagine what we can do…

Theories about learning are great. The one point everyone can agree on is that in order to continue to grow and develop we have to keep learning. There are species of sharks that can never stop moving. Water has to be passing over their gills in order for them to take oxygen from it. I feel that way about us and learning. When we stop learning and developing we get stuck at whatever level we are on and we start to die. Without any new infusion of purpose and learning we cut ourselves off from the water of life. Everything starts to dry up. My favorite book says: "Be renewed with the transforming of your mind."

Napoleon Hill, in his book, "Law of Success," said, "The power to think as you wish to think is the only power over which you have absolute control." I think today I will learn something amazing!

One of the laws of the universe says, "Every living thing is born, grows, levels off, then begins to die." In order to lengthen the process, during the leveling off period, we need to give birth to a new idea, start something new that will begin the growth process. In the absence of this new growth we will start to decline.

This is why the baby in the elevator is so full of life. She is learning. She is growing. No leveling off for her. She is like a rocket headed straight into the heavens. She is already in heaven, because everywhere she looks she is learning.

Learning is vital to life. It is the "growing" stage in the Law of the Universe. Some trees grow for hundreds of years because they have the ability to keep adding new branches and original growth each year. Roses, on the other hand, grow, bloom, and then level off and die either when they are cut, or when they decay on the bush that gave them life.

We are no different. As products of God's divine plan, we can either be like a giant sequoia that grows for centuries, or like roses that bloom, give off a beautiful fragrance and are gorgeous to look at, and soon after, die.

Here is a concept I love. A fulfilled life comes from having desires, goals, and a plan of action to reach them, plus a willingness to put action to your plans, to learn from what you have done and then to give what you learn to others.

It's a formula that's worked for me and that I have observed work for everyone I know who has put it into practice. Maybe it's some of what you will learn today. There are dividends to be found there.

CHAPTER 2
TALE OF TWO SISTERS

Learning in our culture is usually associated with formal schooling. When we're finished with school, we're finished learning—or so conventional thinking goes.

One problem is that many of us conclude from an early age that school is something we have to get through as quickly and as easily as we can. It would be far better if we came to understand at an early age that learning is both a privilege and a lifelong endeavor. It begins with formal education but it doesn't stop there.

From the various email accounts I've had over the years, to my web sites, to the iphone buzzing in my pocket right now—as a plugged-in septuagenarian, I am astounded at how much information I have at my fingertips. I truly do have access to more information than the greatest kings who ever lived, and more than the heads of state of just 50 years ago. (If the presidents of my youth had been able to Google the information available to me today, their actions and decisions might have been very different.) Despite the miracle of the information, and the learning available to us today, we have young people who, despite being adept at manipulating the means for acquiring it, don't go after it with determination or enthusiasm. We have older people, meanwhile, we are too afraid to master the means of getting the information, and therefore they are still living in the time they were born in, rather than these thrilling times of present day.

It speaks to the fact that there are different ways of learning, and depending how we use them, they are more or less effective.

I learned a lot from watching the contrasting ways my mother and my aunt lived and learned throughout their lives. My mother who was born in Armenia, and came to America as a teenager, was the first of six children, and had a totally different philosophy of life from her sisters and brother who were born and raised in America. They had the same parents but the early years of learning were different. It was like different parents raised my mother. Mother had to leave school in the 6th grade, yet one of her four sisters went on to become a teacher with a master's degree. What different paths their lives took, and how different were their ways of looking at and experiencing the world.

Mother raised three children during the Depression, built a wealth of street knowledge through tough life lessons, and was gifted with great insight. This gift would serve her well as ladies and a few men came to her for advice. She would use a deck of playing cards to focus in on the other person's thought process and then proceed to tell them things she perceived about their past and make predications of events in their future.

Her sister, my aunt with a master's degree, was married for a short period of time, and never had children. She was the aunt that would buy dumb things for members of the family at Christmas. In her later years she traveled extensively taking educational cruises all around the world. She was extremely knowledgeable and had a circle of friends she traveled with, but she was never really close to any of them. She found learning and the guiding principles for her life in books and through information. She remained very young at heart and lived to be over 90 years of age. Both women had full lives, each in her own way; one learned from experiences and from being with people, the other from books.

I don't know if learning became a substitute for intimacy in my aunt's life. I don't think she experienced her life as being lonely. But to look at the two women together, my mother was certainly having a juicier, richer time.

The take-home lesson for me was that although my aunt learned many things, they stopped with her. There was no follow-up. She learned, she enjoyed, and that was it. That's why I believe learning has to translate into doing, and doing will lead to true knowledge, and that puts us in a position where we have something to give. My goal is for learning to constantly flow into my life and propel me forward… forward and upward into the heavens like the Elevator Baby.

CHAPTER 3
LEARNING OR REPEATING

There is a theory called the "Peter Principal," which says that a person will continue to grow and develop until they reach their level of incompetence. In other words, we keep learning until we reach a point were we cannot correctly apply the knowledge we learn. In this concept the happiest people are the ones who stop just short of the level of their incompetence. The Peter Principal assumes one can only do one activity and that they are in the profession they always want to be in. Each of us has several areas of life in which we can excel. It's never to late to learn new skills.

When I first started to work for the City of Fresno, my immediate supervisor was a man who had been in his position for 15 years and could not make a decision on any new idea or concept brought to him. One day I made a comment to another higher-ranking administrator about the length of time this man had been in his position. Why did he seem stuck? Was there a problem?

His answer stuck with me till this day. It plays itself out everyday in every walk of life. "He doesn't have 15 years of experience," was the observation. "He has one year of experience 15 times."

The guy stopped learning, and developing. This lesson has served me well. I know that if I keep on learning new ways to do a job, or if I am willing to take a risk and do things a different way, I will continue to grow.

Part of growing beyond the point where things feel solid and comfortable, is connecting the different talents and skills we develop. Another one of my favorite quotes is: "You don't get paid for whom you know, and you don't get paid for what you know. You get paid for when you share what you know with whom you know."

My professional life has been one of continued growth. Very often, there was something that jettisoned me out of a place where I was feeling comfortable. It might have looked like an unfortunate turn of events, but in the end I was always grateful for these upheavals because they catapulted me into a period of new growth it might otherwise have taken me years to reach.

As I look back on my career I see that the average period of time I was in any position was five years. This started when I went to work for the City of Fresno as sports supervisor in the Parks and Recreation Department. I moved to a new position called, Assistant to the Director of Parks and Recreation. And from there I advanced to Building Supervisor for the construction of a new Convention and Sports Center. It wasn't long after I became the special deputy city manger to the mayor. My main responsibility was development and coordination of all Federal Manpower Development Grant money awarded to social and civic agencies in a four-county region. The final stepping-stone in my career with the City of Fresno was to Deputy City Manger. In this position I worked for three city mangers in five years. The path to this professional career included formal education, practical experience working on playgrounds, learning from motivational teachers and volunteering in community-based organizations. It was all valuable. I made the most of every day.

CHAPTER 4
POWER OF LEARNING

In order to not die and add, "Life to your Years" one needs to keep learning. We know this is how we grow. Every living thing is growing, leveling off or dying. Death starts when we stop learning. Physical death of the body can takes years but emotional death can occur at any age. The effect can cause us to shut down and withdraw from life.

I believe that depression is caused when we start to internalize our problems, and stop learning new things or developing talents we are given. My conclusions are based on my observation of people's behavior including two positions where I got to witness and work with people who have mental challenges. My first full time job after college was as the recreation therapist for 5,000 patients at the State Of California's Camarillo Mental Hospital. When working for the City of Fresno, I served as President of the Board for the Fresno County Mental Health Association, and Chairman of the Board of Trustees for the Fresno campus of the San Francisco School of Psychology.

Sometimes mental health problems are purely physical. They can be caused by chemical imbalances in the brain, or other things that can only be solved by changing the state of someone's anatomy, no different than a broken leg or, as with me, a heart that messes up sometimes.

But for quite a few people I've known, mental health problems have to do with not having someone, or some way, to talk about things. Once again, there is learning going in, but it gets stuck. Nothing is coming out and it leads to an overloaded system and before you know it, things start to shut down.

Many of the patients I worked with had significant physical problems, but from my interactions with them, I felt the biggest problem they had was that they couldn't satisfy the most important need we all have: the need for human connection. Each one of them lacked someone in their lives who truly cared about them, and with whom they could communicate. They needed someone to listen to their problems.

Lacking any human connection, many of them had given up on life mentally but had not died physically, and they were upset about it. They were bored and disinterested because life had no more meaning for them.

Shortly after starting the job at Camarillo State Mental Hospital, my recreation classes were so well attended by the patients, and they ran so smoothly that other recreation therapists, all of whom had degrees in the field, wanted to know what special techniques I was using. The head of the department, who had 20 years of experience in the field, asked me to speak about my approach at a special meeting. What I said shocked them.

I told them that my "secret" was to treat the patients exactly the same as I had treated the "normal" healthy people I had worked with in municipal settings outside of the hospital. I used exactly the same approaches, depending on the age group I was working with, as I had in every other place I'd worked. The games and the mixers I used held the same interest for the so-called sick folks as they did for the so-called "normal" people.

The entire experience left me with the simple theory that the only difference between people who are considered sane versus those thought to be insane, is that, "those of us who have others in our lives to share our problems and successes with are considered sane."

Formal education has been studied and proven to be valuable; there is no need to go over numbers here. A formal education can and should continue beyond college. Most professions today require the professional to have some form of continuing education to maintain a license. While in the life insurance profession, for example, the American College presents professional designations to those who pass numerous specific classes. These certifications allow the public to know which agent has what level of education on the subject. When I was in the life Insurance profession for over 10 years and working as regional director of sales and marketing for a large company, I was advised to start taking classes to be certified as a Charter Life Underwriter (CLU). At age 61 I really didn't want to do the studying required. I didn't see the value in getting the certification. But it took me less than two years to pass 10 different courses and receive the prestigious "CLU" designation. It is a privilege to place those letters after my name. It gives me a great deal of pride to do so and helps others know I am a professional in the business. It has also helped me with the requirement that I stay current with continuing education laws. There was value in the learning. However, without putting that learning into action it would have been useless. The experience I gained by doing the work that the designation allowed me to do was the real value. The mixing of formal education with real life experience is where true learning takes place. It doesn't work to take the learning in and let it just sit there.

I heard this quote from a professor while I was working toward a California secondary education certification: "Those who can, DO. Those who can't, teach. Those who can't teach, teach others how to be teachers."

My observations over the years in professional business and government jobs have proven that this statement is very often true. I've run into a number of people who couldn't or didn't want to "Do," and the best way they could come up with something related to what they had learned, was to teach. But lacking that real-world success and experience, they often make the driest teachers.

Some of the best teachers and professors are the part-timers who go back and share their experience with students.

Those teachers who shy away from "Doing," and therefore lack experience should ask themselves this question: "What is experience?" One great definition of experience is that it's what you learn by failing at a task and then trying again, and again until you find a way to make it work.

When did you first become aware of the power of the human mind and its ability to limit or enhance the functions of the body? For me it was May 6, 1954, and I was a senior at Fresno High School. I was the lead distance runner on our championship track team. One day during practice, the head coach, Erwin Ginsburg, came out to our field and announced that a man in England had just broken the mythical barrier known as the, "4-minute mile." Dr. Roger Bannister had run a mile in 3 minutes, 59.4 seconds and he was still alive. His primary occupation in life was not as a runner, but a doctor. I think it was because he was a scientist that he didn't succumb to the popular belief that the human body would collapse if pushed to the point necessary to run a mile in less than four minutes. To prove this barrier was a myth he trained and prepared his body, but he also trained his mind to believe it could be done and that he would do it and live through the experience.

Well, he did it and not only lived to tell about it, but now we tell how he did it. He will forever be known as the first man to run a mile in under four minutes. Since that time, thousands have run sub-4 minute miles and are never mentioned. The world record at the writing of this book is 3:43.13 set July 7, 1999 by Hicham ElGuerrouj, of Morocco. Second place in that same race holds the second fastest mile at 3:43.40 by Noah Ngeny of Kenya. My record time in that same distance when in high school was 4:30.0. This would have put me close to a full quarter of a mile behind the winner had I been in the same race.

My one great college mile experience occurred in 1957 when I was a senior at Fresno State. I was entered in the Special Invitational Mile Run at The California Relays in Modesto, California. Two sub-4 minute mile, world record holders—Tom Landie from Australia and Jim Ryan of Kansas—were set to be together on the same track for the first time. Meet officials needed to fill out the field to make it challenging. Being at the starting line and wishing both of them good luck was the highlight of my college running years. My heart felt like it was coming out of my chest when the gun went off to start the race. For the first three quarters of a mile I was in third place just three seconds behind the two fastest milers in the world. My coach, the great Dutch Warmerdam, the first man to clear 15 feet in the poll vault, was running on the infield yelling words of encouragement. He was more excited than I had seen him in four years. I was known for having a burst of speed at the end of races, called a "kick," and he was hoping it would be there this time too. Would it?

The gun sounded for the last quarter mile. This time I got to witness up front and personal what two sub-4 minute miler's burst of speed looks like. Those two men kicked it in like I had never experienced before. At the finish I was 24 seconds behind, with my fastest time ever, 4:24.0. The winner's time belonged to the man who then held the world record in the mile, the Australian, Tom Landie; he ran, 4:01:3. In second place was Jim Ryun of the University of Kansas with 4:02:5. What a day that was, and what an experience to be running in the same race as the two fastest men in the world.

The next time I became aware of this powerful truth, the mind's ability to control what happens to us physically, was 15 years later.

But first, when I was 15 I was a scrawny kid, just 5' 7" and 111 pounds. My father died of a heart attack a month after I began high school leaving my family with no money and a lot of bills. We lived in a 900 square-foot, two bedroom, one bath house, and thank goodness it was paid for.

I was entering the most prestigious and affluent high school in the county which might not seem like a big deal today, but to an Armenian teenager in Fresno, California in the 1950s, my first day there I felt like I was walking into Buckingham Palace. Ninety-eight percent of the Armenian kids went to Roosevelt High but because of where our house was located, I had the choice to go to Fresno High, where the privileged kids all went. It was considered the better school, so I signed up and walked through those "palace" doors.

Armenians were considered a minority in Fresno in 1950. There were rules forbidding us from buying property within certain boundaries, and that was part of the reason so few attended Fresno High. I knew if I wanted to be accepted there, my only chance was to become an athlete. In time, I could have found my place by falling in with kids who were into the mischief of the day.

That didn't include drugs then, but it certainly included transgressing against the law, and the path from mischief to misdemeanor to prison, all before the age of 20, was well worn, and heavily traveled by kids who started out like me, on the margins of society with a lack of parental support and not a lot of prospects.

My mother was surely determined to do her best, but that didn't include helping me become an athlete; in fact, she had no concern for my social well being at all. She was afraid I would get hurt if I competed against kids twice my size, and that was most of them. She was fifty years of age, had only a grammar school education, her family were all living on the East coast and she didn't know how to drive. When she looked at me all she saw was a skinny, 15 year-old rebellious kid whom she had to raise and depend on at the same time. My brother and sister were both married and living their lives in other parts of the country.

It was no shocker when I asked her to sign a medical release form and pay the $2.00 fee so I could play basketball, and she refused.

Assuming I could talk her into changing her mind, I had other issues. I had no athletic skills. Because I was so small I hadn't been selected for any sports teams in junior high. But my last year there, track was added as a sport and my math teacher, Dean St. John, was the coach, and he made me the team manger. This gave me exposure to the value of athletics and being a part of a team. It didn't do anything for my athletic skill set though.

As a 15 year-old trying to get his life together for high school, I was starting to become aware that I wanted things and that I wasn't going to be able to have them unless I planned and worked for them. No one was going to hand me anything. I began to think of my life in terms of goals and obstacles.

The obstacles to reach my goal were, my skill level, my mother's objection, authorization forms, and money. I had the desire and the dream. In many ways these are the same obstacles that keep most people, maybe even you, from following your dream.

Let's look at the obstacles facing me one at time:

1. Skill level. I had the dream but not the skills. What I heard was… ***"You can't do that. You don't know how."***

2. My mother's objection. Someone else held the opinion that this was not a right goal for me to pursue. This can be especially difficult if the person is someone you respect or love or who holds some sway over you in some way. These voices can be spoken or implied, or we can simply imagine them. What I heard my mother saying was…

"You can't do that. Our people have never done that."

3. Forms and legal paper work often seem like artificial barriers designed for no reason other than to provide discouragement. What I heard the world saying was…

"There is too much red tape to go through."

4. Money. So often, reaching our goals means we have to pay a financial price. How often have you heard a voice saying…

"That's too much money. You can't afford it."

The last chapter of this book will give you the opportunity to do your own evaluation of one of your goals. For now, know this is true: When your desire is strong enough, when you know your dream is worthwhile, and you set your mind on accomplishing the task, your body will follow.

My desire was to be accepted by my classmates and athletics seemed like the best way. During one of the regular physical education classes I asked Coach Ginsburg if I could go out for the track team. He asked if I was fast. "No," I said sheepishly.

"You don't look like a shot putter or discus thrower. What do you think you can do?" he asked.

"On my way to school, I can run farther than everyone else before I get tired," I said.

"Good," he said. Hearing him say that one word was a very small beginning. But sometimes that can make all the difference.

The intramural track meet is this coming Friday, he continued, and he said he would enter me in the lowest division for the 660-yard run, which was the longest distance of any of the races. I felt like this was his way of finding out if I had what it takes to make Fresno High's track and field team. I placed second in the race but the kid who won the race was a smoker and got so sick he never wanted to run again. His decision not to try out for the team left me as the top 660-yard runner in the lowest (Class C) division.

It was official: I was a member of the Fresno High Track and Field Team. The reward was a Block "F" sweater which as far as I was concerned, announced to the world that I was an athlete.

The dream was coming alive. I was so excited I decided to try out for the basketball team; their season began in the fall and winter, which was before track even started. They didn't have many boys my size and miraculously, I made that team too.

Now that I was on these teams the next challenge was figuring out how to overcome the obstacles mentioned earlier. I needed the parent authorization form signed, money for a mandatory medical exam, and I had to figure out how to keep this secret from my mother. I saved most of my lunch money to cover the cost of the medical, and then forged my mother's name to the authorization form. It may have been wrong to sign her name and not tell her but a "No" from her would kill my dream of being accepted. So I figured it was better to ask for forgiveness than permission. Pardon, the pun, I was off to the races. Literally.

It was tough attempting to explain why I came home late from school or where I was going on nights we had basketball games. During track season some of the meets were on Saturday afternoons and that meant I had to do all my yard work and whatever else Mom wanted done so I could be at the meets. It is amazing what we can accomplish when everyday tasks stand in the way of something we really want to do. I was learning how to overcome obstacles and I didn't even realize it.

During the next three years I was blessed to earn two Block "F" letters in basketball and in varsity track.

In 1953 I became the first student in school history to earn a Block "F" varsity jacket in Cross Country. With this accomplishment I also earned a lifetime pass to all Fresno High sporting events. This award was only given to students designated as an "all-around athlete," by lettering in three different sports. There were two other recipients the year I graduated and both were three-year varsity lettermen in football, basketball and baseball, outstanding athletes in every sense of the word. Accepting this award during graduation and standing next to these two schoolmates was the highlight of my high school years.

Athletics did prove to be my way to acceptance. A bonus for not giving up on my dream was a track scholarship to Fresno State College, where I continued my formal education. I also earned a lifetime pass to all Fresno State athletic events by earning a Varsity "F" letter in track each of my four years. All these years later, it's surprising to find how much those accomplishments still mean. I've done many things that resulted in my being more well known or making good amounts of money. I've accomplished things that took longer to achieve and which opened more doors. But those early accomplishments, from which we learn what it takes to make our dreams come true, stay with us for a lifetime.

CHAPTER 5

LESSONS FROM ADVERSITY

The biggest lesson learned from all this participation in athletics came after one of my biggest defeats. It was in my first year of running and I had won races against two other city high schools and was the city champion. I had recorded the fastest time for the 660-yard run in the county!

It was time for the county meet and I was favored to win.

During the race I was in front of the field of 20 runners with about 75 yards to the finish line. In the next few seconds my life changed dramatically.

Someone came along side of me, then another was on the other side and a third right behind me. The finish line is getting closer now, the runner on my right moves a little in front, the one on my left bumps me and the one behind goes around me. The finish line is right there and suddenly the race is over. Five of us reached the finish line within seconds of each other. The result was that although I was favored I didn't make it into the top three and received no medal or points for the team. I came in fifth. Within 75 yards I had gone from first to fifth, from champion to "also ran."

Did I see this as my fault? No! I was pushed. The judges didn't see it correctly. The others should have been disqualified. Surely I was in the top three! I had run the best time prior to this race. I was the favored; I was Arsen Marsoobian!

This was my story after the race. I was complaining to the judges, telling my story to my teammates, or anyone who made the mistake of asking what happened. The only one who was absent from all of this drama was my coach, Erwin Ginsburg.

Monday at school I was still complaining and explaining to everyone who would listen how I was cheated. Finally Coach called me aside. This is what he said.

"Arsen, I don't ever want to hear you say one more thing to anyone about that race. I was at the finish line and the judges got it right. You where fifth because you Quit! The first time someone bumped you, you quit. There was less than 10 yards to the finish line and you led for 99 percent of the race. You were running easily, no one was challenging you and the race was yours. But at the first sign of adversity you gave up and lost what should have been yours, and your teammates'.

"If you ever quit in any race again you will never run for Fresno High School again. From now on your race is five yards further than anyone else. You have to go beyond what you think is expected of you if you want to be a winner."

Then he turned and walked away. It has been over 60 years since I learned that lesson and you can rest assured the quotation is correct. I can hear him saying all those words to me as if he said them yesterday. From that point on I lost very few races, and I was always running harder than any other competitor when I crossed the finish line.

One loss came at the end of my junior year at the City Track and Field Championship. Fresno High had won the City Cup, awarded to the winner of this meet by the local newspaper, three years in a row. By tradition, the cup moved from school to school, depending on which school won the city meet. But if we could win it for the fourth straight year we would get to keep the cup permanently—our school would own it. It was a great goal but it wasn't going to be easy. We had lost to each of our rivals, Edison and Roosevelt, in dual meets earlier that year. Although only one meet stood in the way of us getting to keep the cup forever, it didn't look good.

The morning of the track meet Coach Ginsburg held a team meeting. He was obviously trying to motivate us. The talk he gave us was right out of a movie script; I can remember the day and hear his voice like it was yesterday. Holding the cup up over his head, he said, "This is only worth a few dollars; not very impressive. But it's been ours for the last three years. If each of you do your best you could be the team that makes sure it never leaves Fresno High." During the talk he outlined how he thought we could still get enough points to win. Part of his strategy was moving me up to the varsity—I was just a junior and had been running all season as part of what we called the, "Class B" team. I had never competed in a Varsity race. He said he had scheduled me in both the Class "B" and varsity half-mile races; he would decide at the meet which one he wanted me to run. The Class B was run just before the varsity, and I was predicted to win it. However, my best times were not close to the older, stronger varsity runners. Roosevelt High our cross-town rival had two varsity half milers who had finished one and two in every race they had run for two years. I can still remember their names: Ed Moon and Elmer Placios. If they did the same in this meet they would win enough points for Roosevelt to make it almost impossible for us to overcome with the remaining races and events.

I repeatedly asked Coach which races I would run but he kept answering, "I don't know yet." With the start of the class B half-mile just minutes away I still didn't know if he was going to move me up, so I reported to the starter. I was getting my lane assignment when Coach came running up, pulled me aside and asked, "Are you ready to run with the big boys?"

My knees where shaking and my stomach was turning, but I looked at him and said, "I can do it." He told the starter Marsoobian's going to run in the varsity half-mile. Take him out of the Class B race."

Everyone at the starting line was surprised and confused at what was happening. Then the announcement of the last-minute change came booming over the stadium speakers, "Arsen Marsoobian will be running in varsity half-mile." It all happened so fast I had no time to think about or understand what was going on. I was going to become a Fresno High School varsity athlete.

The race got started and for the first quarter mile I was happy just being close because the pace was a lot faster than I had run before. As predicted the two Roosevelt High School runners were in front as we started the final quarter mile. I don't remember just how far back I was going into the last 200 yards, but coach's voice came back to me: "We don't quit at Fresno High." I got up on my toes and started a full-out sprint passing Palcios with less than 50 yards to go, and finally Moon at the 885-yard mark. The problem was the finish line was at the 880-yard mark. I had finished second in a Fresno High School varsity record for the half-mile with a time of 2:03.06. Ed Moon's winning time was 2:02:5.

The points for this surprise upset and second place finish were enough to tip the momentum and we went on to win the City Championship and retire that cup to the Fresno High School Warriors trophy case where you could still see it today.

That was a full day of learning for me. What I learned was you never know what you can accomplish until you begin; and to never give up; and to always finish strong.

It didn't matter what happened in the first 680 yards of that race, my best was yet to come in that last 200 yards. After that, I was known as the kid with the fast finish.

My challenge to you if you feel like you are somewhere near the last 200 yards of your race is, "Are you ready for a great KICK to the end of your life?'

It's been said by many people its not how you start that counts but how you finish. The point is, it's not too late. Your life isn't over. Retirement need not be the finish line. You can still do what is in your heart or feel like what you are meant to do with your life. Later in the book you will have the opportunity to go through a question and answer format to actually discover what you have a passion for and what you can accomplish.

For now, think about these questions: Have you ever gotten close to a goal but given up because some adversity came your way? Or was there another lesson you needed to learn to make you a champion? What was it in your past that stopped you from doing or becoming something you think you might be able to do? What was the setback that caused you to stop trying? It's never too late as long as you have the desire to do or become the real you. Go the extra five yards and be ready to, "run with the big boys." Trust me—it's worth it!

CHAPTER 6
LEARNING BEYOND THE CLASSROOM

I n 1964 at age 29 I joined the Optimist Club in North Fresno. This was a group of men who had supported a youth program I was responsible for as part of my work. One component of our meetings was to have speakers on any number of topics. It was a wonderful experience to listen to these people.

One day a speaker came to the club with a message and program that would change my life forever. He was a local children's TV personality, Jimmy Weldon, and he talked about personal desires, setting goals and how to accomplish them. His approach came via a program called "The Dynamics of Personal Motivation (DPM)." This approach was explained on seven cassette tapes and came in a package with a tape player and a manual; I remember it all came in a business case. The cost for the magic in the box was $600.00. To put that number in perspective, I was earning $388.00 a month before taxes and I was married with three children all under the age of five. Yes, I bought the tapes with the understanding I would get $100 for each referral that resulted in another sale of the program. My net results were that I sold three packages over the next three months, so I cut the cost of my package in half.

I followed the directions rigorously. They were to listen to tape one for six days before going to the next tape. Day One—listen with no distractions and makes notes. Day Two—listen in a quiet place. Days Three to Six—just play the tapes and do normal activities. Listening to the tapes became like listening to music on the radio. I turned on one tape every morning while getting ready for work. I played it over our home intercom system so my three children had to hear it. They may not have consciously listened but it was going in their little brains anyway.

The results were dramatic. The following changes took place in the next two years. I received a promotion from the City of Fresno Parks and Recreation Dept. to the city mangers office, with a special assignment to administer the mayor's federally funded Manpower Program. I was selected by a service organization called the Jaycees, as Fresno County, "Outstanding Young Man," of the year and it led to my being recognized the following year as one of 1,600 "Outstanding Young Men of America." The award was based on professional growth, leadership and community involvement. It was an award I had wanted, and in fact, I had written it down as a goal. I was certainly not a shoe-in to win it and I was struck at the time by the obvious connection between the fact that I had declared to myself that it was a goal, and I had written it down, and the result that I had won it. I absolutely connected the two events. I felt like I had discovered a new power in the universe.

I bought a new house, was serving on seven charity boards within the Fresno community, some as chairman; I held leadership positions in Optimist International's governing structure. All of this came from learning about the Dynamics of Personal Motivation and the confidence it gave me to act on what I was learning.

The downside to all of this was a divorce from my children's mother. As I was growing in my professional and personal life she was raising our children and not interested in listening to or participating in the personal growth programs. We started to have different dreams and desires. I had seen the value of goal setting and the process to unlock one's potential and wanted to share the message.

The divorce and all the drama surrounding it caused major shifts in my life. I took what turned out to be a big gamble. My 23-year career with the City of Fresno came to an end when I accepted the position as executive director for Fresno State University's independent athletic boosters program called, The Bulldog Foundation. What I thought was a great opportunity ended after just one year when the power brokers inside the organization didn't renew my contract. No one could say I wasn't doing a good job for the foundation —in my year on the job I increased the volunteer workforce by 100 men.

I was 15 years out of high school and yet it was the first time since I lost the race in which I was bumped, that I felt like a loser. Coach's "Don't you ever quit," lesson came to mind. Emotionally it was a tough period in my life, but I made a conscious choice not to sever times with that organization and to continue to show them what I was made of. The lessons on the DPM tapes had taught me success was measured by what I did and not by what others thought. Pulling on these two strengths, I was in the top 10 overall fundraisers in the Bulldog Foundation each year for the next three years. The first year after not having my contract renewed I finished third out of 300 volunteer boosters.

However, I needed a means of earning an income. I logically thought I should look into the possibility of teaching others about some of the lessons I was discovering. I thought the life-changing process of developing ones own personal plan of action, setting goals and moving forward… all these concepts seemed tremendously valuable and I felt like I had learned enough that I could share them.

I knew a man who had purchased the local DPM franchise and was speaking and selling the program. When I approached him about possibility of joining him he made a strong case that it was hard to make any money in the business. Then why was he in it, I wondered? In time I understood that he was telling me I could not speak well enough to motivate others to action. His opinion of my ability caused me to start losing my self-confidence. It was hurtful and tested my own beliefs and my confidence in my ability to use the information I had learned to create the things I knew I was capable of.

I took it all in and doubled down on my self-confidence. Within a few weeks I was hired as a salesman for a large local printing company. I was happy to land the job but it didn't take long to figure out this was not going to be my life's work. Especially when the owner told me over lunch, in a very condescending manner, "This is what you will be doing for the rest of your life." I didn't feel the need to tell him that one of my goals was to own my own business.

I knew this was not the time or place to quit. The race was barely half over.

By now it was March, 1980 and I was being recruited into the life insurance profession by the largest local life agency, "New York Life Insurance Company." I decided to embrace the life insurance profession by applying what I had learned about goal setting and personal motivation. With that decision, my climb back to the top was started. How high I would go was up to me and my attitude, and not affected in any way by the opinions of other people.

In a period of 10 years, I went from the All-American dream of being married to a great wife, having three great children, owning a big house with a pool, driving a Cadillac, holding positions of leadership in the community, and a top position in city government, to being out of work, going through divorce and having a personal life that was a total melt down.

But somehow, I never gave up on my belief that I was a winner and that as long as I kept my faith, stayed close to my children, was willing to learn new things and continued to give back to my community, I would always have a full and successful life.

What is your story? We all have one. If you gave up on a dream or was discouraged from the task you wanted to do, it's not to late. It's a terrible feeling to get to climb the ladder of success, and then realize your ladder was against the wrong wall. If you're like me as I am today at age 77, and you feel like you are in the last lap of the mile race that is your life, it's time to get up on your toes and start the KICK to the finish line. "We don't always win every race in life, but we never quit," says Papa Soob.

CHAPTER 7

THE ROLE OF FORMAL LEARNING

**Learning doesn't really start
until you think you know it all.**

W hat do you want to learn? What is the next thing you need to learn to move your life forward? To answer these questions, you might begin by looking at the areas of your life that excite you the most, places and activities that push your "enthusiasm button," no matter the circumstances.

Think about when you learned the most in school? It was probably when you were interested in the subject and wanted to be in the class. At what grade did this happen? First, fifth, ninth grade? In high school, college, postgraduate classes? Maybe it was after formal school, like on the job, classes for the profession you're in, or were in. Let me share my story.

When I was in school it was hard to know why I was there other than the insistence of my parents and the law, which said I had to be. The most fun and learning came in physical education classes. What were the main lessons?

How to get along, team work, competing for what you wanted, motivation, social skills, reward based on your effort in accomplishing a task, discipline, honesty, winning and losing, leadership and respect for others.

When high school was over I wasn't sure what I was going to do with my life. I had done several odd part time jobs to earn money from the time I was 12 but none looked like a career path. For two summers my friend Bill Eaton got me a job working as forest ranger to help fight fires in the national forests located in northern California. At the end of the summer of my senior year, not knowing what I was going to do, I went to visit my sister in New Jersey. Maybe I could find work there, return to my roots and live with my cousins.

Then a letter arrived from Flint Hanner, the head track and field coach at Fresno State College, offering me a "work aid scholarship," to enroll in school and run for Fresno State College. When I received the letter, school had already been in session for two weeks and Coach had to pull some strings to get me into classes. Once formally enrolled I had to pick a major course of study. The process required a visit with the counselor, an aptitude test to find out where my interests were concentrated, and help determine the best course of study for me to pursue.

After a short period of time getting to know each other and talking about the track team, the school counselor said, "You're Armenian, aren't you?"

I said I was.

"Then I think you should be a business major because that's what Armenians do. My assistant will help you find which classes are still open in that major and get you started. Good luck, to you. Your coach says you have a lot of potential."

I never got to take the aptitude test. My ethnic background was all the advisor thought he needed to know about me.

By the end of the first two semesters I was on the brink of not qualifying for the track team. I was falling like a hundred pound boulder that was pushed off a tall building. I was going to crash into a million pieces and lose everything unless I made some changes. Coach Flint Hanner had a conversation with me and we switched my major to physical education. Athletics was what I had been interested in all along. Also, if I majored in physical education it allowed Coach to keep track of my classes and grades. The grades became top priority. It was the first time I had to be accountable to someone other than my mother.

To get started on the road to eligibility I took a three-unit summer school class on Chinese history. It was the only class available in my time schedule. The professor was Chinese and spoke with a heavy accent, which added to the drama. I made it through with an average grade. The first semester of my sophomore year my academic load consisted of a maximum of 15 units at Fresno State College during the day, and a 3-unit two nights a week music appreciation class at Fresno City College. My overall GPA came up to an acceptable level allowing me to make the track team, but I had missed the cross-country season.

The other piece of the story during that semester was the income side of my life. To earn the scholarship I had to do different jobs around the school's athletic department. It only paid $50 a month and I needed more money to pay my bills so I also worked as a handy man for a flower shop, as a playground leader for the City of Fresno, and a basketball official for the City of Fresno's adult municipal league. This was the year that I started to grow up and started giving life to my years.

When was your turning point? Have you found it yet? It is never too late to start to learn what you are truly interested in. You will also be amazed how easy and quickly it will come to you.

Yes, I did graduate with a B.S. in physical education in four years. I was on the varsity track team all four years and was a recipient of the lifetime pass to any and all athletic events conducted by Fresno State athletic department (which I still use to this day.) The next year I received a California secondary education certification, making me eligible to be a high school coach and teacher. I did not become the Armenian businessman the college counselor had decided I should be. As the great speaker,

Les Brown says: "Other's opinions of you do not have to become your reality."

I would add, "Most of the time, they probably shouldn't." To thine own self be true.

What did you study after high school? Is there any connection between the subjects you studied and the job or profession you are making your money from today, or yesterday? If you're like most people, they don't match.

The match I believe it's important to create is between what is in our hearts and what we choose to manifest with our hands. The days when I am living true to what is in my heart, are the days when what I produce has the most value and gives me the most satisfaction.

Two questions to contemplate:

Have you been pushed or allowed yourself to be influenced by others' opinions or assessments of you, into making choices that turned out to be not the best for you?

Are you doing something with your life and your time that is not what excites you but is based on ideas or conclusions you made a long time ago?

PART TWO: THE UNIVERSAL TRUTH OF BODY

CHAPTER 8

SUIT UP–YOU'RE IN–YOU CAN DO IT

Applied knowledge is power.

My favorite book says, "Faith without works is dead." Werner Erhard said, "Understanding is the booby prize."

I'm not afraid of much in life, but the thought of not acting on the things I know to do, and want to do, truly scares me. I have often thought, "Get in action, Arsen. Not taking progressive action on your thoughts will leave you with empty dreams."

My favorite definition of success was written by Earl Nightingale, and I have edited it slightly. Earl Nightingale said in a talk called, "The Strangest Secret," which was a major influence of the blockbuster 2006 self-help film, "The Secret." Earl Nightingale said, "Success is the progressive realization of a worthy ideal."

It's the root of a definition that has become a mantra for me: "Success is the daily progression toward a predetermined, worthwhile goal"

Let's look at this definition a little closer.

First, the word, "success," is often measured by the final outcome of an event or project or predetermined goal. However, this definition implies that success is in the process not the end result. The word, "daily," implies you need to be working on something everyday that is moving you closer to your goal. I love the next part because it sets the definition apart from others you may have read or heard about: "Predetermined worthwhile goal."

This means a goal is thought out. You know where it fits with all the other goals in your life. The doing of one activity doesn't counteract the achieving of another goal. You may have a goal of making a million dollars, but without coordination you end up a divorced millionaire with ulcers. In order for it to be a successful goal it must be, "worthwhile." If your goal is to be rich and famous and the only way for you to accomplish it is by killing 10 people while robbing a bank, this would not be a "worthwhile goal." The results would be there but you would not be a success.

Every great inventor will tell you that he tried and failed several if not hundreds of times before he was successful. They were doers, and had, "I will not be denied," attitudes as they worked toward their predetermined and worthwhile goals. Everything we have in our lives now was first started in the mind of one person who was willing to take action on his or her thoughts. Not taking progressive action on your thoughts will leave you with just empty dreams. My favorite book starts out with this process. First came the thought, then the plan, then action. God thought, and then spoke, and then it was done.

Learn something, anything, with your mind and then make it happen by doing. It is much better to start and take a chance on success or failure than to not do anything and be sure to fail.

If we go back to how children learn we find most tasks are taught by doing. They learn to walk by doing it, not by our telling them how to walk. You could show them videos of how people walk but unless they try and fall down a few hundred times they'll never walk.

We spend the first five years teaching our children to stand up, walk, talk, and learn. We spend the next fifteen years telling them to sit down and shut up.

In one of the speeches given by Theodore Roosevelt in Paris, France in 1910, here is what he said about the importance of "doing":

"It is not the critic who counts; not the man who points out how the strong man stumbles, or where the doer of deeds could have done them better. The credit belongs to the man who is actually in the arena, whose face is marred by dust and sweat and blood; who strives valiantly; who errs, who comes short again and again, because there is no effort without error and shortcoming; but who does actually strive to do the deeds; who knows great enthusiasms, the great devotions; who spends himself in a worthy cause; who at the best knows in the end the triumph of high achievement, and who at the worst, if he fails, at least fails while daring greatly, so that his place shall never be with those cold and timid souls who neither know victory nor defeat."

This statement doesn't only apply when you are in the work environment. It applies to every aspect of your life.

Especially when you move into that retirement mode. Most seniors want to be the critic, the spectator, not the risk taker in the game. They don't know how much is lost by settling for that comfortable chair outside the arena.

Finally, take a moment to get some paper and write down the answers to these questions. Think of areas in your life where you are sitting in a chair and not playing, where you are outside the arena instead of inside on the court or the field of play.

What would you do if you were not in that chair? What would you do if you got out of the chair and into the game?

Write down your answers and let them take root in the rich soil of your life.

CHAPTER 9

THE VALUE OF DOING

Just Do It.

—NIKE

A favorite word used by coaches when asked about their team's performance is, "execute." If they have won, they did it well; or if they lost, the players didn't execute well enough.

At the professional level players spend hours prior to games looking at videos of their opponents, studying their skills and their techniques. They have specialty coaches to correct and teach proper methods to help them play a particular position. The overall strategy is put on paper, studied and learned by everyone associated with the game. Goals are set. Expectations are high going into every game. Everything has been learned. Then the game starts and the Doing comes into the equation.

When the game is over the results will always depend on how well each team executed what they learned during their preparation. The next time you watch any college or professional game, listen to what each coach says when asked to evaluate the game. The winning coach says "Our guys really executed our game plan today." The losing coach says, "We just didn't get it done. Players didn't execute the plays. They didn't play up to their potential today." Success is in the doing.

It is good that the potential is there. If the execution is performed correctly enough times, then you start to become what you have learned. It is in the Doing that we become who we want to be. Professional athletes in every sport get selected and paid bonuses based on their potential. How they execute as they use that potential will determine who they become (and if they ever get a second contract). It will also determine what they will be able to give to others.

One of the most recognizable symbols in the world is the swoosh from Nike, the sports shoe, clothing and equipment maker. Do you remember the legendary Nike slogan? "JUST DO IT." Now all Nike needs to do is show the logo and we all know the name of the company, the slogan and what it means.

The man who started Nike did so by putting his product in the back of his car, driving around to college and high schools all over the country, showing and giving away his brand of athletic shoes. Up until this time the Converse shoe company had the athletic shoe business all tied up. If you wanted the best on your feet it was Converse. The Nike shoe proved to be a better product and style. A coach friend of mine tells a story about how he was offered shares in the company for just a $2,000 investment. He turned it down because it was an unknown back of-your-car operation that many people thought would be broke in a few years, if not sooner.

Here was a man who believed in what he had built and decided to "Just Do It." Most of us will not be given bonuses for our athletic potential but it doesn't mean we can't execute using our talents. In the universe of recreational sports there are many activities to choose to be involved in: bowling, golf, fishing, tennis, softball, basketball, running, weight lifting, dance, swimming, biking…. Just pick one, or add one of your own. Get off the couch today! Nothing adds years to life and life to years like exercise.

Bowling is big business today and seniors are a huge part of that sport's revenue stream. A friend I used to play golf with convinced me to bowl in a summer league with him on Wednesday afternoons. It had been at least five years since I last bowled in a league, but I figured, why not? An afternoon break in the middle of the week could be good for me. Besides there will be a lot of old people in the league so I should be able to keep up. Well, as I write this, the summer league is almost over and these old people have been kicking my butt all over the place. The league is called Sexy Seniors. It is a mix of men and women from 60 to 90-plus years of age. Most have some kind of health issue but it doesn't matter. They are out doing this terrific activity and enjoying being with one another. I am sure our group has more fun than any other group that uses that bowling alley all week long.

A couple of ladies, who are legally blind, play with 10lb balls with five finger holes and average 140 per game. There is another lady who has bowled for years, is in her 80s and has a 185 average and routinely rolls 200-plus games. There are two men in wheel chairs; one guy has to use a cane to walk from his car to the lanes and at age 85 I saw him put down his cane and bowl 250.

It makes me ask, "What could we all do if we put down our 'canes?'"

At my country club some years ago, there were several players over 80 who scored their age on regular basis. I was lucky enough to play and win a couple of senior events, but I was the kid at 70.

I have another friend, Tom Marsella, who at age 70 plays on a national championship senior baseball team. In 2010, Tom won the low hurdles for the 70—74 division at a national senior track event.

The U.S. record for the mile run by a male over age 75 is 5:57. That's 90 seconds off my personal best. Maybe it's time for me to buy a new pair of running shoes and get out there.

The point is you don't have to be a world class, speaker, CEO of a company, or a president of a rotary club to be adding life to your years. Just start by doing something that you like to do. It's time for each of us to suit up and get in the game of life!

"You don't have to be great to get started but you do have to start in order to become great," says keynote speaker and author, Les Brown.

CHAPTER 10
THE RETIREMENT LIFE INCLUDES DOING

In February of 2001 my wife of seven and a half years filed for divorce and in March of that year I returned after an 11-year absence to my hometown of Fresno, CA, to start a new chapter in my life. I was apprehensive about returning to the community I was raised in and where I accomplished what felt like a lot in my younger years. I held it as a challenge and so it became one.

I had left after making a quick decision to accept a position as regional sales and marketing director for a large life insurance company. Taking that position meant moving to the New Jersey shore area and working all over the East Coast. During the coming 11-year period I would have 15 addresses and live in nine cities in three states. I would also meet my wife and her three wonderful children, all of whom were teenagers at the time and all of whom I came to love as if they were my very own.

But now it was 2001, I was closing the book on that section of my life and returning to Fresno to begin another. My return kicked off a period of uncertainty and reflection. The divorce was a major financial and emotional blow and knocked me off my base of comfort and confidence. I felt confused and I didn't know what to expect next. I was particularly troubled to not know what I would do professionally. I didn't know whether I should return to simply selling life insurance, or seek work with the City of Fresno (although I hadn't worked there in 20 years), or perhaps, I thought, I should become a Wal-Mart greeter.

Eventually I did become an independent life insurance agent again. Although I wasn't passionate about it, it felt good to be doing something I knew I could do well.

I didn't give any thought to what I really wanted to do with the rest of my life. Looking back, like many people in their 60s and 70s who don't have a clear idea about what they want to do—what they want to learn and accomplish and give away—I was secretly preparing to die. I didn't think of it that way, but when I look back, that's what I was doing. As the saying goes, I wasn't buying any green bananas.

In this period of my life, I was doing whatever came my way. Have you ever gone through a period of your life where you let whatever circumstances came your way determine the thing you would do next? It's a reactive lifestyle, not proactive. I realized I had lived more of my life like that than I realized—reacting to circumstances and then making the best of whatever came next.

After watching me drift like this for three years, on Father's Day, 2004, my younger son, Bryan and my daughter-in-law, Julie, surprised me with a membership in their country club where the main activity was playing golf. I realized what they were giving me was the gift of retirement. I was 69 years old. I was grateful and I embraced it.

I studied the game of golf in books and videos, I took lessons, I bought a lot of equipment and I played all the time. My scores got better. I set goals for myself to win tournaments. I eventually set the club record for the most rounds played in a calendar year: 174. I was making new friends. I was a golfer. It was a dream come true for a 70 year-old guy. How could life get any better than this?

Right?

Then one day I received a phone call from a lady who represented a charity based in Seattle, Washington. We had met a few years earlier while I was developing a charitable life insurance program for churches and not-for-profit organizations. She was calling to recruit me to join her in representing a company selling software that would help people pay off their mortgages in one-third the normal time. It was a new network marketing company and she offered to help me learn, and get clients, so I signed up.

After about a year of working with this group, I attended the national convention in Atlanta where the keynote speaker was the well-known author and developer of the "Chicken Soup For The Soul" series, Mark Victor Hansen. He gave a motivational speech on the value of the company's product and all the lives it was touching.

At the end of his presentation he had a special offer. Those who purchased his pre-packaged program on internet marketing would also receive tickets to attend a three-day seminar of speakers in Los Angeles featuring a roster of some of the most successful and dynamic speakers in the country. Several of us who were working together bought the internet marketing program, thinking, in addition to its value—learning all about platform speaking—it would be a good opportunity to meet again. When the time came to go to the seminar only two of the six of us actually made it. It turned out to be a three-day selling fest with each speaker giving good information then selling his or her, "how-to seminar." The visions of being a motivational speaker came back, which gave me a feeling of excitement and hope that maybe that dream wasn't dead.

The feelings were so overwhelming, in fact, that I found myself in the back of the room signing up for one seminar after another. Ever since the days when I purchased my first set of inspirational recordings, I had a desire to be a public speaker. Now I could feel that dream taking hold of me, and I felt moved to pursue it. One of the seminars offered covered two full days in Las Vegas and was reduced from a cool $15,000 to just $2497.00. I wanted to pursue this course of learning and that meant soaking up everything about it as quickly as possible. (I was, after all, the guy who shot 174 rounds of golf in one year attempting to master a game that has brought iron-willed men to their knees in mad frustration and tears.) This was more exciting to me than any golf shot I'd ever hit. If life could feel like this, maybe I'd start buying green bananas again.

In addition to registering for all these programs is was the first time I met Lynn Rose. She had a booth promoting her,

"WOW Factor" Seminar and selling her musical CD'S. More about Lynn's impact on my life later.

One of the programs I purchased was a week-long seminar on presentation and platform skills by a international speaker named, Chris Howard. On the last day of his seminar, another speaker made a surprise appearance: Les Brown. After listening to Les for about 10 minutes I was certain he was someone with whom I wanted to study the art and the business of public speaking, and I registered for a seminar he was teaching. Then I went home and slammed headlong into a brick wall of doubt. What was I thinking? I was in my mid-70s, not my mid-20s. I had a resume' of heart attacks, not public appearances. I was a retired life insurance executive with a respectable golf handicap and one foot in the grave; I had never written a bestseller or led a great personal growth seminar. I'd never won an election, made a fortune, led an army, acted on screen or been a professional athlete…. why would anyone listen to me? How could I be a speaker when I probably had nothing to say?

I called Les Brown's company and left a voice message saying I was backing out of his seminar and would someone please refund my credit card. I called several more times and left messages, but a few weeks later my card had still not been credited. My hands were getting clammy because it was almost time for the event. Then my phone rang. It was Les Brown himself.

After agreeing to refund my money, Les spent the next 45 minutes on the phone with me. What had changed my mind about the seminar, he asked? I started with a string of negative thoughts I assumed he would agree with; they seemed very real and reasonable to me. I was much too old to pursue something new like public speaking. It would take me 30 years to achieve success, and I didn't have that long. Even if I did have some success, it would mean more travel than I was willing or able to do. No one would care what I thought or had experienced or felt I had to offer. It was a long list of reasons.

Then this world-renowned speaker spent the next 45 minutes on the phone with me reminding me how badly I wanted to pursue my dream. At your age, he said, you have a wealth of experiences to help others on their journey. Was my dream really not worth two days of my time and a little bit of money, he wanted to know? Finally, he said something to me, a line for which he is famous: "YOU

HAVE GREATNESS WITHIN YOU." He believed it, and I could feel it. That did it. I was refocused and I did spend two days studying with Les.

When I finished with him, I was almost ready. A short time later I enrolled in an intensive course with the multi-talented teacher and performer I mentioned earlier, named Lynn Rose. Lynn is known for her ability to inform, motivate and inspire large groups of people all over the world. Her course is called, "The WOW Factor!" because it inspires participants to take the kind of action in their lives that leaves them and everyone around them with their mouths open, saying, "WOW!"

Near the end of Lynn's course it was obvious to me I was ready to conclude the formal learning portion of my development and get on with the "Doing." I knew like it was time for me to get up on stage in front of an audience and talk about my life and experiences in a way that would inform, entertain and inspire people. But that didn't mean I felt ready.

The thing I was certain about was that it was time to leap; what would happen after that, I couldn't know with certainty. If you think about the times in your life when you extended yourself greatly, when you stepped forward and for the first time put your feet down on brand new ground...can we ever know we are ready for something that new and challenging? I surely was concerned I would make a fool of myself.

Then I raised the stakes and made it 10 times worse. I decided my first major talk would happen in my hometown in the civic auditorium whose construction I had helped supervise. What's more, I would take responsibility for selling most of the tickets and I would make a big night of it; I decided to invite several of the friends I'd made from my studies as a new speaker, to share the stage with me. At first, the date I chose was my 75th birthday—the night would be a birthday party I would throw for myself—but when all the schedule coordinating was finished the big night was set for a few weeks later, March 24, 2010.

The "doing" or "action" part of life is the critical piece of the puzzle. Think back for a moment about the things you have accomplished in your life. Would any of those things have happened without some action taking place? Now think of all the ideas, projects, experiences that you wanted to do but told yourself you could not. Are you still waiting for some of those things to get done? Wasn't a lack of action the reason it never got accomplished?

I have wanted to write a book for a long time, but until I started, the actual "doing" of sitting at the computer and starting to type, was something I thought about often but never did.

The action part of life is where experience comes from. You cannot get experience without acting on any subject or idea you have learned. The world is full of individuals who have great knowledge but no experience. They are just half full and most are modestly successful at best. However, the really successful people who give us most of the things we enjoy in life are the ones who have taken action on their ideas. Many fail at the action the first or second time. Some have failed hundreds of times before they were successful.

There is a story about a well-known man lecturing at a major university. One of the students asked, how did you get to be so successful? He answered, "Because I have experience."

The student then asked, "Where did you get the experience?"

"From my failures," was the answer. You can only get experience when you are willing to take action. Then you learn from the outcome.

The doing or action part of life is the critical piece of the puzzle. Think back for a moment about what you have accomplished in your life. Would it have happened without some action having to take place? Now think of all the ideas, projects, experiences that you wanted to do that you could do that are still waiting to get done? Wasn't the lack of action the main reason it never got accomplished?

For those of you who are older, consider this question: What is the attitude you are going to take into the last stage of your life? Sit around complaining and waiting for the end to come, or suiting up and getting back in the game of life? I'll bet you want to look back on your life and say, "I'm glad I did," and not, "I wish I had." Making sure the task is real and attainable is critical to the process. Take the time to go through the process listed at the end of this book. As you venture out to places beyond where you currently think, or have thought in the past, that you would ever be able to go, I bet you will create some fantastic things.

When I participated in Les Brown's "The Power of Voice" workshop in June, 2009, I was just a few miles from UCLA Medical Center, where I had lain on death's doorstep 10 years earlier. I wrote and practiced and learned how to tell that story, "The Old Man on His Deathbed," as one of my assignments at the workshop.

On March 24, 2010, the show went on. It was titled "The Time Of Your Life—IS NOW," because it was held in the William Saroyan Theater, named for the Fresno-born author of the Pulitzer Prize-winning play, "The Time of your LIFE." Having had the privilege of meeting and spending time with Mr. Saroyan, I was thrilled to make my first professional talk in the theater with his name on it.

On that night, I took the stage in Fresno along with several of my friends, including the incomparable Les Brown and the amazing Lynn Rose. I don't know if I was ready, but I absolutely gave it everything I had. All the speakers connected with the audience that night. I remember hearing the crowd still buzzing as they left the auditorium, having heard seven speakers lay bare their hearts and tell their truth about life's struggles, accomplishments and beauty. Lives were changed that night, as they always are when the great speakers take to the stage to tell the stories that show us to be real and make us whole. One of those changed lives was mine.

CHAPTER 11
THE PROOF IS IN THE DOING

In a book by Howard S. Friedman, PhD, and Leslie R. Martin, PhD, entitled "The Longevity Project," the authors expose some of the myths about living a long life. The study they talk about began in 1921 and was led by a Stanford University psychologist named Lewis Terman. It followed the lives of 1,500 people for over eight decades. One of the myths was, "Taking it easy adds years to your life."

Here is what they found on this subject. "Continually productive men and women lived much longer than their more laid back comrades. A sustained work life mattered a great deal more than even their sense of happiness." Wow!! They go on to say, "Giving up an interesting, demanding job to live in a golf community away from you friends could actually increase the risk to your health."

In another myth, "Jocks outlive nerds" they state, "Being active in middle age is the key. And exercise doesn't have to be intense, like running long distances. Dancing, tennis, bowling, golf, and gardening will also work. The important thing is to find activities that suit you and stick with them over the long haul."

What is the alternative to doing, and what are its consequences? Earl Nightingale said, "The man who can read and does not is no better than the man who can not."

He is saying if you have the ability to do something and you don't do it, you're just like the person who has no ability. If you are just a spectator in life sitting around the house playing games on the internet, you are no better off than the person who is paralyzed and can't get up.

I had a very close friend who was a decorated War World II prisoner of war. He was a happy-go-lucky guy, married to a lovely lady, with two sons. He had a good job and he was respected in the community. He spoke publicly about his war experiences to civic groups. For years, he led an organization that put on an air show which recalled some great airplanes and pilots from World War II.

Then he retired from the job he loved for more than 35 years and in retirement he started to withdraw from community life. Soon, like me, he had heart bypass surgery. After the tragic death of his oldest son he gave up completely. From that time until his death some 10 years later he spent his days, reading, watching TV, smoking his pipe with a glass of wine or two in a makeshift room in the garage.

He was left to himself in his solitude with a housekeeper to watch over him. In less than a year the housekeeper found my friend dead in his bed. He chose to sit life out just as though he was confined to a cell in some far away land. You don't have to be good to get started but you do need to get started to be anything.

Here is another study that confirms what I am saying on the subject of living life to the fullest.

An Australian woman named Bronnie Ware was a caregiver to many in their final days before dying. She became close with many of them and said that each was able to find his or her peace before passing on, some sooner and others later. Her memoir about her work with the dying is called, "The Top Five Regrets of the Dying—A Life Transformed by the Dearly Departing." Her book is a memoir of her own life and how she was transformed by the regrets of dying people. (Bronnieware.com)

This excerpt is with Bronnie Ware's permission. Here is some of what she says about the end of life and regrets.

People grow a lot when they are faced with their own mortality. I learned never to underestimate someone's capacity for growth. Some changes were phenomenal. Each experienced a variety of emotions, as expected, denial, fear, anger, remorse, more denial and eventually acceptance. Every single patient found their peace before they departed though, every one of them.

When questioned about any regrets they had or anything they would do differently, common themes surfaced again and again. Here are the most common five:

1. I WISH I'D HAD THE COURAGE TO LIVE A LIFE TRUE TO MYSELF, NOT THE LIFE OTHERS EXPECTED OF ME.

This was the most common regret of all. When people realize that their life is almost over and look back clearly on it, it is easy to see how many dreams have gone unfulfilled. Most people had not honored even a half of their dreams and had to die knowing that it was due to choices they had made, or not made.

It is very important to try and honor at least some of your dreams along the way. From the moment that you lose your health, it is too late. Health brings a freedom very few realize, until they no longer have it.

2. I WISH I DIDN'T WORK SO HARD.

This came from every male patient that I nursed. They missed their children's youth and their partner's companionship. Women also spoke of this regret. But as most were from an older generation, many of the female patients had not been breadwinners. All of the men I nursed deeply regretted spending so much of their lives on the treadmill of a work existence.

By simplifying your lifestyle and making conscious choices along the way, it is possible to not need the income that you think you do. And by creating more space in your life, you become happier and more open to new opportunities, ones more suited to your new lifestyle.

3. I WISH I'D HAD THE COURAGE TO EXPRESS MY FEELINGS.

Many people suppressed their feelings in order to keep peace with others. As a result, they settled for a mediocre existence and never became who they were truly capable of becoming. Many developed illnesses relating to the bitterness and resentment they carried as a result.

We cannot control the reactions of others. However, although people may initially react when you change the way you are by speaking honestly, in the end it raises the relationship to a whole new and healthier level. Either that or it releases the unhealthy relationship from your life. Either way, you win.

4. I WISH I HAD STAYED IN TOUCH WITH MY FRIENDS.

Often they would not truly realize the full benefits of old friends until their dying weeks and it was not always possible to track them down. Many had become so caught up in their own lives that they had let golden friendships slip by over the years. There were many deep regrets about not giving friendships the time and effort that they deserved. Everyone misses their friends when they are dying.

It is common for anyone in a busy lifestyle to let friendships slip. But when you are faced with your approaching death, the physical details of life fall away. People do want to get their financial affairs in order if possible. But it is not money or status that holds the true importance for them. They want to get things in order more for the benefit of those they love. Usually though, they are too ill and weary to ever manage this task. It is all comes down to love and relationships in the end. That is all that remains in the final weeks, love and relationships.

5. I WISH THAT I HAD LET MYSELF BE HAPPIER.

This is a surprisingly common one. Many did not realize until the end that happiness is a choice. They had stayed stuck in old patterns and habits. The so-called 'comfort' of familiarity overflowed into their emotions, as well as their physical lives. Fear of change had them pretending to others, and to their selves, that they were content. When deep within, they longed to laugh properly and have silliness in their life again.

When you are on your deathbed, what others think of you is a long way from your mind. How wonderful to be able to let go and smile again, long before you are dying.

Life is a choice. It is your life. Choose consciously, choose wisely, choose honestly. Choose happiness.

What about you? When given the choice between Doing and Watching, which will you choose?

Life is a lot more fun being in the game. As that great American Philosopher, Yogi Berea said, "It's not over till it's over."

The evidence is overwhelming. Doing is always better than watching.

CHAPTER 12
DOING AND ADVERSITY

It was Thursday morning June 30, 2011, a nice warm day in the city of Fresno. I was up at 6 a.m. and off to the gym for a quick morning workout. Before leaving I checked to see if my blood pressure was in a safe range where I could go for a workout. I had been having issues with it being too low for the past month. It was border line so I went.

Once at the gym I went through my routine of 5 to 10 minutes of stretching, five minutes socializing with a couple older Armenian ladies who keep trying to get me back to my roots by speaking to me in Armenian. This particular morning only one was there so I joined her, walking on the treadmill next to her, talking and listening for 10 to 12 minutes before going to work on the strength training machines. Our conversations must sound funny. Her English is better than my Armenian but still broken. My Armenian isn't what it was when I was younger. Add to this the noise of the gym and my not wearing my hearing aid. Neither of us probably had any idea what we were saying, except for our ability to communicate and interpret using big gestures—hands and eyes. It felt like mixing learning with doing.

After about 45 minutes on the machines doing a variety of exercises I started to feel a little tightness in my chest. I walked around, talked to few people then I took a seat in the lobby before leaving for home. By the time I arrived home, just a few minutes from the gym, I was feeling better. I started cleaning up around my apartment and made a breakfast of dry cereal and an English muffin. I went to my computer to check emails and plan the day. During this short time my vision started to blur and I could feel my heart beating. The tightness in my chest was coming back. Given the events of the past month with my heart I decided to check in with my doctor at Kaiser Hospital. Through a series of phone transfers I ended up talking to a nurse and doctor in the E.R. going over my symptoms. My big mistake was to say the two magic words, "chest pain." They don't understand, "a little tightness."

The next question came, "Can you get to the ER"? Sure, it's only a 5-minute drive for me.

"No, can you get someone to drive you?" I will try but if not I can get there.

"No, we will send an ambulance. We don't want you to drive." Ok, I said, I will let you know. My daughter-in-law, Julie, was willing to come get me so I avoided the embarrassment of an ambulance ride.

When we arrived at the hospital, my son, Bryan, was just walking up from the parking lot. We hugged and kissed and put our arms around each other and walked into the ER. I said those two magic words, "chest pain" to the admission lady and went straight to the head of the line. It wasn't worth it, not like dropping a famous name and getting a great table in a restaurant. The minute you find yourself being slotted into that system, your freedom, privacy, confidence and sense of yourself as an individual who matters to the outside world, starts to disappear. I do not mean to sound ungrateful. On the contrary, I owe my life to some terrific, lifesaving doctors and nurses who are very, very good at what they do. But feeling your life pulled out from underneath you is a terrible feeling and it leaves you thinking, "Do whatever it takes to stay healthy. Losing your health is terrible." All those bad habits, however much fun they may or may not have been….. they're not worth it! Eat well. Go to the gym. Learn about living a healthy life; then do it. Become one of those sharp people who loves it. Cherish and defend your good health.

By 2:15 p.m. the E.R. doctor comes in and says, "It doesn't appear to be anything serious but we think you should stay the night, so we can make sure."

Doctor, I have places to go and things to do, I insisted. My grandchildren are dancing at their annual recital. This is the last night.

"Well, its up to you," he says, "but if you leave and something happens to you it could be your last recital".

Doctor, there is something else. I am writing a book with the title, "DON'T DIE." If anything happens to me before it gets published it could hurt sales and ruin my reputation!

He laughed and said I had just proved his case. He was more committed than ever to proceed cautiously. With that I was admitted to the hospital and he went to order more tests.

If you are reading this, then you know I made the decision

to stay for the evening and have the tests, all of which were negative. My heart was fine this time. The mystery of reoccurring tightness in my chest continues to this day.

After the final blood draws for the evening I was wide awake. I flagged down a nurse as she was walking by the room and requested something to write with. She was kind enough to get me several sheets of plain white paper and a pen. It was time to start doing by taking advantage of the quiet time by writing accounts of the day and writing notes for the book. My thought was, I could work with my mind while my body rested. Doing does not always have to be in the form of physical activity.

When given the opportunity to be a spectator or a participant you are always more alive when you're the participant. Don't be content to sit on the sidelines and watch the world go by until its time for you to say good-bye.

You may be accumulating years, but do those years have real life in them? My favorite book says, "Faith without works is dead." I say life without doing is dead.

There is a statement I heard when I was new to the life insurance profession: "Nothing happens until someone sells something." Everything we have in this world may have come from the thoughts and minds of a human being. However, until it gets explained, designed, built and sold, it is just an unfulfilled dream. Our lives work the same way. You can have a lot of knowledge but until you take action on that knowledge it's of no use. Earl Nightingale's quote is worth repeating here. "A man who does not read is no better than a man who cannot."

I don't know why things happen the way they do. Maybe if the cause of the chest pains that sent me from the health club to the hospital that day had been discovered, I would have thrown in the towel. Instead, that day only served as a wakeup call that got me going on writing this book you are reading right now.

But a year later it was a different story, so to speak. Still trying to find the source of my occasional chest pain, gifted cardiologist Amir Sanati, M.D., found a 100 percent blockage in one of the original grafts that had been done on my heart back in 1999. However, the doctors I was working with were hesitant to operate because of all the previous procedures I had had. I have quite a bit of architecture and not a small amount of metal holding my sternum together.

I could have accepted that opinion, that I was too fragile to undergo more surgery, and gone forward gingerly with my life, but I didn't. Dr. Sanati referred me to a heart surgeon named Dr. Arthur Lee who agreed that my case was tough—he referred to operating on me as his, "Super Bowl,"—but he was ready and confident to go for it. "It was me against that blockage in your heart, and I wasn't going to lose," he said.

Once again, I believe God guided me to one of only a handful of surgeons who could have successfully done this operation. When it was over, Dr. Lee mentioned that I had three other arteries with 90 percent blockages. I went back to him a month later and he finished his work. Within days I was back playing golf, and pain free. It is a special, deep and curious relationship between heart patients and our surgeons. As I write the final words of this book, I am remembering, Dr. Lee is waiting for his signed copy.

CHAPTER 13
DREAMS ARE FOR DOING

The worst feeling in the world is to have an idea, take no action, and then watch as someone else becomes successful with the same idea. In 1979 I was the first person I knew of to write down rules to a game my friends and I were playing by creating imaginary teams of National Football League players. Each week we would pick an imaginary team of NFL players who were competing that week, and share our rosters with the other fantasy players in our imaginary league. In the game, our imaginary teams scored points based on the real-world performance of our players that weekend.

I wrote the rules down and called it "MARS FANTASY FOOTBALL." I even went so far as to get my rules legally protected, printed and advertised so that others who wanted to play could sign up and join. When I didn't get any response to my adds I became discouraged and did nothing more with the idea.

Then one day in 1993 I walked into a store and saw a magazine with the title, "FANTASY FOOTBALL." My first thought was someone had stolen my game. I checked with an attorney and learned the statute of protection for the copyright had run out, and I could not prove that I was still working on developing the game. My blockbuster idea was gone and the price for the lack of confidence in my creativity, and for my lack of action, is knowing that today more than 22 million people play fantasy football and the game is a multi-billion dollar industry.

I know some of you are older and you might think, as I did when I was telling Les Brown I wanted to throw in the towel, that it's too late to act on some of the ideas and ambitions you have. Please know this: it is never too late to start pursuing you passion or dream or idea. If it takes learning new skills or learning more about a subject, then get started right now. "Ships are safe in the harbor, but that's not what ships were made for."

If you are agree with me that it's important to take action on your dreams but you are snagged by the idea that the ambition tugging at your soul is too big, then remember this from Daniel Burnham, the architect and urban planner of the city of Chicago, who said, "Make no little plans; they have no magic to stir men's blood and probably themselves will not be realized. Make big plans; aim high in hope and work, remembering that a noble, logical… (idea) once recorded will not die, but long after we are gone be a living thing, asserting itself with every-growing insistence. Remember that our sons and our grandsons are going to do things that would stagger us."

I love the last part because it plugs us, and all of our deeds, big and small, into the grand context of what our ancestors did and what our successors will do after us. Knowing that you are part of the huge wheel of human progress, how can you ever drop out? You can't. We are all part of it and we just do what we can do, our very best, and we must give it every day.

Take the action steps to get the knowledge, and then do what it is you need to do. If you don't, it will forever be a dream. Or worse, you will watch someone else live your dream. The last chapter is set up to help you explore the different interests you have, and pick one or two that will add life to your years.

My brother Pete Marsoobian was fourteen years older than I so I didn't know much about how he grew up. The other day I started reading the autobiography he was writing when he passed away in Oct. 2004. He never finished writing his interesting life story. However, let me share what I learned from his writings.

My brother Pete had a dream to be a Jazz musician from the time he was around 12 years old. He was growing up in little town called West New York, New Jersey. This was 1932 to 1936 right in the middle of the Great Depression. Pete was the oldest son of two Armenian immigrants. Dad was uneducated and working hard making a living as a barber. He was also a disciplinarian who didn't understand dreams. My brother's dream of becoming a jazz musician was not something our father was inclined to support. For Pete it was movies, music, anything in the entertainment world that got him excited. He was so determined to follow his dream he dropped out of high school at the legal age of 16. He got a job during the day and gave all the money to our father to help support the family.

However, at night he was going to places where jazz music was played. He was learning and developing his skills. He learned to play the drums so well that during the World War II, even though he enlisted within months of the start of the war and was in until it ended in 1945, he never left the States. He kept getting moved from one base to the other with the dance bands for officer's clubs. He was also in the marching band as a drummer. His dream became a reality and he played up until a few years before his passing. Most of his lifelong friends were musicians. Many became famous or played in big bands through out the 40s and 50s.

You may not recognize my brother's name from his musical ability. However, you have probably enjoyed the food he made famous: pancakes and Belgium waffles. No, not just any pancakes but the ones at IHOP (good old "International House of Pancakes.") Yes, this high school dropout and jazzman, used his talents to go to France and attend the famous Cordon-Bleu Culinary School in Paris. Pete played drums in jazz bands all over France so he could live and pay for his classes. He even ended up marrying the young French girl whose parents rented him his apartment. They were still married when he passed away.

You'll never know how fulfilling your dream will impact the lives of others. Pete had a full happy life right up until the end. He added life to his years and did the same for the people who knew and loved him. I loved my brother and I deeply miss him.

Think of him on your next visit to IHOP. The pancake chain got its name because Pete wanted to showcase the different ways pancakes could be enjoyed. Here is how it all started.

My brother was working for two Jewish brothers who owned a coffee vending company in southern California. Pete was in charge of getting all the coffee made and ready for delivery every morning. The two brothers asked Pete if he would help them fulfill a dream they had to open a restaurant specializing in pancakes. They asked him to use his skills from cooking school to create better pancakes. My brother thought they were nuts but agreed to give it a try. He baked and they ate pancakes for over a year before they had what they knew were the best pancakes they had ever eaten. The brothers approached their father with the idea and requested a loan to get started. He thought they were nuts but agreed to loan them the money to buy a small piece of land and to build their fancy "house," and decorate it with a lot of foreign flags in the windows. The young Armenian chef with a cooking degree from a French cooking school started cooking pancakes at the first, "International House of Pancakes" in the summer of 1958. The restaurant sat on a triangle piece of property across from Bob's Big Boy Restaurant and just a few blocks from NBC Television studios.

The cost of the land and building was around $70,000. Pete was given the choice of being either a partner or the head chef. Having been raised during the Great Depression his thought was to play it safe and just be the head chef. Besides, he concluded they didn't know anything about the restaurant business and would probably be broke in a year or so. Years later when they where growing and I asked if he was a partner he told me of his decision. I was shocked. How did he think two Jews and one Armenian were going to go broke doing anything?

In the first month they were so busy my brother was working 16 to 18 hours a day making his secret formula dry mix. Several nights it was easier to just sleep in the restaurant than drive the Los Angeles traffic and run the risk of being late.

By end of first month the brothers knew their dream was going to be realized. They had enough profit to pay for the land. During the next 26 years they took their crazy idea of a restaurant that specialized in serving mainly pancakes from around the world to a worldwide company that was trading on the New York Stock Exchange. They also made sure my brother was well compensated even though he was never a partner. In early years Pete was awarded three gold medals for his original pancake batter.

As a side note, I worked as dishwasher for a summer in the original store. It was the only time my brother and I worked together.

PART THREE: THE UNIVERSAL TRUTH OF SOUL

CHAPTER 14

KEEPING WHAT YOU GIVE

WHAT YOU GIVE YOU KEEP FOREVER.
WHAT YOU KEEP YOU LOSE.

W hen I first heard this quote it didn't make much sense. How does that work? Give it away yet keep it forever? How do you lose anything if you keep it?

The dictionary defines GIVE in several ways.

1. To pass on or hand over
2. To hand over to another to keep
3. To cause to have
4. To be the source of
5. To part with, sacrifice
6. To say or state, utter
7. To perform, present
8. To yield or move because of pressure or force

When you look at the above quote in the context it was used, it makes perfect sense. The giving was not of material possessions but of oneself for a cause. When a coach tells the players before the game, "What you give you keep forever," he is referring to the ability of each player and his (or her) willingness to give all of that ability away. If they do, they will keep positive memories of the event forever. However, if they keep the ability for themselves they will lose the opportunity to build positive memories of the event. As you can see, giving is more than the sharing of material wealth.

My favorite book says," What you give will be given unto you seven fold."

It is important to acknowledge that we can't give away anything that we do not own. To give advice we must have knowledge of the subject, otherwise our opinions have no value. There is little value in giving advice if the teacher has no more knowledge than the receiver. We see this in every day life. Golfers with a higher handicap give advice on mechanics of the game to someone who is a better player. One toddler can't give another toddler advice on how to stand up and walk.

The true value in giving, as we get older, is sharing our knowledge and experience with the younger generation. Hopefully this information will translate into ways to make their lives better.

If our wisdom is kept it will be lost, but by giving it away it will live on in lives of others long after we are gone from this planet. My favorite book also says, "it is better to give than to receive."

CHAPTER 15

ATTITUDE OF GIVING

The conventional worldview says, "Get all you can and keep it." It's reflected in the famous bumper sticker from the 1960s that says, "He who dies with the most toys wins." That's a lie.

The real JOY in life comes from GIVING from the heart. It will make you younger in mind and spirit. I don't know all the medical terms but there are endorphins released from the brain that make us feel good. The better and happier you feel the longer you live, and the longer you enjoy life. No one can lengthen one's life, however, you can add life to your years through the act of giving.

Unfortunately many people die at age 35 or 45 and don't get buried until they are 70 or 80 years of age. They die with all their desires, talents, ambitions, gifts and dreams still in them. They died full and lived empty. My friend, Les Brown says everyone should, "Live full and die empty."

There is a story of a man in his last stage of life, lying alone in a hospital bed. In a weak state he opens his eyes and sees several figures standing next to his bed. Oh! My high school buddies came to visit me, he thinks. "How nice that you have come to cheer me up," he says in a whisper.

Then one of the figures, a tall one, leans over the bed, takes his hand and says, "We are your, dreams, talents, desires, gifts and ambitions that you never used. We didn't come to cheer you up, WE CAME TO DIE WITH YOU."

When I first heard this story it made an impact on me because in December 1999, I was that old man in the hospital bed recovering from 13 hours of quadruple bypass surgery. I could have taken my crew—my talents, desires, dreams, gifts and ambitions—to the grave with me had it not been for God's grace and the team of doctors and nurses at UCLA Medical Center. It was my second heart surgery in 70 days, and it was performed on my 65th birthday. For the four days in the intensive care unit I had a nurse either in my room or sitting just outside the door, around the clock. During the first few days while I was in this heavily drugged and exhausted period, I had a strange experience. When I closed my eyes there was a figure of a man dressed in black with a goatee type beard calling me.

I could sense my spirit moving toward him though a dark shadowy passage.

However, when I thought about the specific people who said they would give up prayers for me, little crosses would appear and be so bright they would light up the room and take away part of the darkness. When my son Bryan would come in the room, several illuminated crosses would surround him.

Some people came in the room and brought the darkness back. This continued for the first 72 hours. Then on the morning of the fourth day, after a very vivid dream, I felt like I was to pick one of three people and request that he or she say out loud, "I love Jesus." One of my three choices was my Armenian night nurse who I believed was trying to kill me. She was the one I knew I must select to make this declaration.

When the time came for the nurses shift change, I called her over to me and asked if she knew Jesus. She said, yes, and told me she attended the Armenian church.

"Good," I said. "I would like you to say out loud, 'I love Jesus." She laughed and started to walk away without saying anything. I raised my voice insisting she make that statement. She asked me to calm down, came over, held my hand and said, "Yes I love Jesus."

The moment she said it a brilliant light occurred eliminating the darkness and the dark figure. In that moment calmness came over me, and I had the assurance that I was given a new life! At the time, I didn't realize I was being given another opportunity to use whatever talent, hopes and dreams God has entrusted to me. It has been several years since that time and much has happened in my life, not the least of which is learning to be a speaker, to share my story, and to be moved to write this book.

Let me share a personal story about the joy of giving and how it gives back.

On the evening of February 3, 2011, I was given an opportunity to give or sell an object that was priceless to one person and has monetary value to many. The object is a major league baseball. It is the ball which former major leaguer, Matt Williams hit in 1994 to break the record for most home runs before the All-Star break. It was 28th home run of the season. As fate would have it, the players went out on strike that summer and at the All-Star break the season was over. This made Matt, Major League Baseball's Home Run leader for 1994. As faith would have it, my stepson went to that game at Dodger Stadium with the young man who lived next door to us.

The neighbor boy caught Matt's historic ball as it cleared the left field wall and sailed into the third row and smack into his mitt. When they came home, so excited, they told me about the event. I offered to buy the ball from him if he would write out all the particulars of the historic event, with the time, place, and how and when it happened. We agreed that the price for the ball would be $30.00. Both boys signed and dated the hand written note, and the ball became mine.

The ball traveled with me for 17 years through 15 moves around the country. Over the years I often thought about how to contact Matt Williams to see if he would buy it from me. Then I learned that on February 3, 2011, Matt Williams was to be guest speaker at the annual Baseball Hot Stove Dinner in Fresno. Matt was a player for the San Francisco Giants when he set the record. My son Bryan's good friend, Mark Gardner, a former teammate of Matt's and now the Giants' pitching coach, was also a guest at the dinner. Mark was gracious enough to introduce me to Matt before the program started. I was finally going to get an opportunity to ask him what he would pay for the ball. Within a few minutes of conversation with Matt Williams I knew I was to GIVE the ball to him. Several people who sell memorabilia said the ball had value, and if I got it autographed by Matt with the date of the event on the ball, its value to collectors, would dramatically increase.

In my short conversation with Matt I realized the ball had meaning beyond money to him. I asked him if he would like it and he smiled said, "I would be proud to display it in my home trophy case. Are you giving it to me?" Without thinking I said, "Hell, you hit it, not me." With that I handed him the encased ball, with the handwritten note attached. With a big smile he shook my hand and said, "I really appreciate this and will not forget you. Thank you."

What happened next is the message from this story. When Matt started to speak to the large crowd of young and old baseball fans he told the story you just read. He then publicly thanked me for what he called a, "wonderful act of kindness," and he said he would never forget his visit to Fresno, California, and his time with us, great Giant baseball fans.

The smile and happiness from Matt Williams, the current part owner of the professional baseball team, the Arizona Diamondbacks, and a potential future Hall of Famer, was worth more than any money I would have received from sale of "THE BALL." Who knows, it may end up in the Baseball Hall of Fame, in Cooperstown, NY. Giving is so much better than receiving. That small act of GIVING will live on in Matt Williams's life long after I am gone, as well as being a very special moment for me.

My youngest son Bryan, who is a San Francisco Giants fan, captured the moment on his iphone. Bryan is a part-time assistant baseball coach at Buchanan High School, which has had nationally recognized teams in recent years. Bryan was also a student coach at Cal State Fresno when another career Giant was a player there, former major league pitcher, Mark Gardner, the bullpen coach for the 2010 and 2012 World Series Champion Giants teams.

Think back for a moment at all the times you gave of yourself, or a material object that made another person happy, or maybe a word of encouragement at just the right time. What was that feeling like for you at the time? Sadness or Joy?

I bet it was joy, and it brings a big smile to you right now as you relive that moment in your mind.

My experience tells me that the secret to joy in life comes from giving. Your life cannot be full when you spend it just accumulating people and things in your life. The bumper sticker should read," HE WHO DIES WITH ALL HIS TOYS GIVEN AWAY, WINS"

Another reason to GIVE is so you will have room for more of the better things and experiences, which brings us full circle to learning and its importance.

We learn so we can DO, and we do so we can GIVE. Giving is one of the best ways to add life to your years. The act of giving also requires you to look outward and not inward to your problems. When the main topic of a conversation is who has the worst illness or the most unsolvable problems, you know the aging process has reached an advanced state and the participants are barely alive. Those in this conversation may be "living" but there is very little life to their time.

CHAPTER 16

TOUCHING LIVES AND GIVING LOVE

This point was most clear to me when I observed my 82-year-old mother as she was recovering from a cornea transplant eye surgery. This is the same woman with a sixth grade education mentioned in an earlier chapter. When she was in her early twenties a man told her she was gifted with psychic abilities. She explained this talent simply as the ability to tell individuals about their past and give advice on events that could occur in the future.

She would have five to ten women a day come to her home for her to lay out 21 regular playing cards and talk for 30 minutes to an hour. She would make coffee; some would bring pastry of some sort, or fresh fruit. She had no price for the time spent but if they happened to leave money on her table, which she would "find," she never complained. If they couldn't afford anything it didn't matter, they all got the same time and advice based on what was coming to her as she studied the arrangement of the cards. Since she didn't drive a car and had a hard time walking, some of the regulars would take her shopping or to visit friends. She would leave me notes so I knew where and when to pick her up. She had a flamboyant personality. She was always the first to pick up a tab, bring gifts when she visited anyone, and always dressed up when she went out. Mother was the life of the party. She was a graceful Armenian dancer right up until she passed on at age 88, in March 1987.

After her eye surgery, when the doctor found out she lived alone, he suggested she move to a nursing home for a few weeks, as she needed more assistance.

When she got into the nursing home environment and the nurses treated her like the other older patients, I noticed she was willing to just lie in bed and do whatever she was told. I watched this for about two weeks and noticed she was giving up on life, worrying about her health and wondering when she was going to die. She said her eyesight was failing and she couldn't read cards anymore. She thought it was better if she just stayed there in the home with the other old people and not be any trouble to anyone.

In talking with my sister we worked out a schedule to help

her and to get her back home. She was in a state of depression by this time and giving up. We got our mother home in her environment and sure enough the ladies started to come by to see "Betty," her professional name. She couldn't read for them but most of them didn't care because they loved the motherly advice she handed out when they shared their stories and problems with her over coffee and pastry. Within a week, I noticed she was looking and sounding like herself again. She wanted to start cooking and baking and moving around the house more. She started to look forward to getting back to reading the cards. "The girls need me. You know they have such tough lives and so many problems," was how she saw it.

Yes, Betty got back on her feet within another week or two of being home. She went on serving the ladies until 1987 when she suffered a stroke at the age of 88. Mother put up a tough fight for about three weeks going in and out of hospitals, and then one night she slipped into a coma.

The days following her passing I stayed at the house and answered the phones that rang all day and night. Conversations went like this: "Is Betty available to talk to me tomorrow?" No, I am sorry Betty passed away on

March 22, 1987. "What? How did that happen? What am I going to do now? How will I know what to do when I have a decision to make?"

"Pray," I told them. "That's really what Betty did for all of you. Thanks for calling."

While at the house I found an old ledger type book, with a rubber band around it. It contained the first name of the ladies, the day, time they came, and amount of money they left. Most were under five dollars and the largest was $20.00. The total for the last year was approximately $3,000. The way she gave her time and money away to others made everyone in town think she was making $30,000 a year.

Her giving attitude added life to her years, and brought hope, insight and happiness to many, many others.

CHAPTER 17
AGE MAKES NO DIFFERENCE IN YOUR GIFT

Walt Whitman, a wonderful American poet and philosopher, wrote: "From this hour I ordain myself loos'd of limits and imaginary lines. Going where I list, my own master, total and absolute. Listening to others, and considering well what they say. Pausing, searching, receiving, contemplating. Gently but with undeniable will, divesting myself of the holds that would hold me. From this hour I ordain myself loos'd of limits and imaginary lines."

What he is saying is that all of us have an inner force that will draw to ourselves whatever we need and most deserve. The last two words are the biggest stumbling blocks to adding life to years: "imaginary lines."

What imaginary lines have become barriers to what you want to achieve, or are keeping you from doing what you want to do? Is there a little voice that says things to you like, "People my age don't do that" or, "No one in my family has ever done anything like that."

Here are some others:

"Retirement is for relaxing and doing nothing."

"My health is too bad to do anything."

"The cost is way too much for me."

"My friends would laugh at me."

"I don't have any formal education. School was always hard for me."

"I'll probably die soon anyway."

I know this list, because I also have used all of them at one time or another in the past several years. Those of us born before 1948 have been conditioned through conscious and unconscious messages to believe that after age 65 the purpose for life is relaxing, sitting around do nothing, or maybe traveling to see how the rest of world is living, or lived. We call it retirement.

Go ahead add your own list. Now sit back and look at the list and see which ones have held you back from living your desire and purpose in your Life. Here is the good news. "IT'S IMAGINARY." You can cross the lines and move into a new reality any time you want. If you need permission, I am giving it to you right now.

Earlier in this book I told the story of an old man dying

and getting ready to take to the grave with him his dreams, talents, gifts and ambitions which he had never acted upon. I have never forgotten the impact that story had on my life. An impact that has caused me to do what I am doing right now—writing this book in hopes it will have some impact on your life.

As you think about new goals, the temptation will be to base them on your current circumstances or past experiences. Don't let this determine your further destiny. There is something in all of us that is greater than the circumstances we are facing. Put your thoughts on what you want to do, not on what you don't have.

What would be a goal you would set if you believed you would not fail? The last chapter has tools to help you set realistic, worthwhile goals. Come join me on the other side of the, "imaginary lines."

THE BONUS

One solution to the challenge of "imaginary lines," is a formula I learned years ago from one of the many motivational programs, which I have used to give direction to my life. Hopefully this process will help you put the pieces together and give you courage to cross those imaginary lines. This will take some work on your part, but the results will, "add life to your years." Complete the process for all the major areas of your life (mental, physical, family, social, spiritual and financial.)

In the world of real estate this question is commonly used to establish the value of a piece of land that is for sale. It is, "What is the highest and best use for the land?" The asking price will most likely be based on the answer to this question.

Similar questions when looking at our lives are, "What is the value of your goals? What is the highest and best use of your time, talent, and energy?

The person I know who was most at ease answering these questions, was Ronald F. Wagley, my friend and former boss at Transamerica Life. Ron went home to be with the Lord on July 21, 2012. I will always be grateful for his guidance, loyalty, support and friendship.

It had been several years since our last visit but the news of his passing hit me hard. He was doing much of what I write about in this book—giving life and meaning to his years.

He was a learned man, he loved playing golf, and he was a massive giver on every level. When his life ended in the back of an ambulance, he was living full out. He and his bride of 50 years, Soni, were conducting a Bible study in their home at 7 a.m. on a Saturday.

I don't believe there was any part of his life where he would have said, "I wish I had." The rest of us whose lives he touched will always say, "I am glad he did."

At the memorial celebration of his life, "Ron's Philosophy," which he penned in July, 1982, 10 years before he would become President CEO and Chairman of the Board of Transamerica Life, and 30 years to the month before he died. Here is "Ron's Philosophy:"

As I grow older the more I realize how rapidly my life is passing before my eyes. Time is like a well-greased string, which slides through my taut fingers. I've tried vainly to hold it or even slow its pace, but it only accelerates year by year. Just as surely as the past 40+ years evaporated so quickly, the next three or four decades will soon too be gone.

So there is no better time than now to assess the values that are worthy of my time and effort. Having made that evaluation, I have concluded that the accumulation of wealth, even if I could achieve it, is an insufficient reason for living. When I reach God's time to call me home, I must look backward on something more meaningful than the pursuit of money and things; nor are fame, position, prestige or title of any lasting benefit. I will consider my earthly existence to have been wasted unless I can recall a loving family; a consistent investment in the lives of people; and a genuine, earnest attempt to serve God. Nothing else makes much sense, and certainly nothing else is worthy of my life's investment.

—Ron Wagley

Now it's your turn. Get blank pieces of paper or a blank page on the computer and answer these questions:

1. What do I really want to do or have, now and for the balance of my life?

2. If answer to #1 is really true, why am I not doing it, or why don't I have it?

3. List all the reasons you are not doing or having what you want. (This will provide you with the list of activities you will need to reach your goal.)

4. Develop a realistic time line to complete each activity listed in #3.

5. List the sacrifices it will take in terms of your time, changes to lifestyle, finances, etc. for each activity.

6. Answer with total honesty this question. "Is what I listed in number 1, worth the cost listed in number 5 to accomplish the list of tasks in number 3?"

7. If your answer to the question in point # 6 is YES, then get started because it is all but accomplished. You know where you are going, you know what you want, you have a plan of action and a time line to get it done. Congratulations, you have a predetermined worthwhile goal and if you work toward it on a daily basis, you will succeed in achieving it.

8. If your answer to this question is NO, discard the paper you have been writing on because the dream you were thinking of is only a wish. It has very little chance of becoming a reality. This is the difference between a realistic attainable goal and a wish.

I hope this helps you clarify the goals that will bring joy and prosperity into your life, and eliminate the frustration that comes from not reaching goals you think you want.

"The Giving," goals should be the easiest to identify and achieve because there are so many ways you can give. We covered many of them earlier with examples and stories. "Giving" can be as simple as helping a neighbor with a task, volunteering for your favorite charity or religious organization, being a mentor or tutor to younger people, etc. You complete the list. You could give money if you have it but that's just one part of giving. However, most people focus on it when the subject is mentioned. The ultimate gift is giving the very best of who you are to others. It has been said, "What gifts and talents you have are gifts from GOD. What you do with them on this earth is your gift back to GOD."

Remember well this question: ***Do you want to look back on life and say, "I'M GLAD I DID" or "I WISH I HAD"?***

Take time to go through the goal developing process. Then step over those IMAGINARY LINES and into LIFE.

DON'T DIE
Keep living with PASSION and PURPOSE
YOU WILL HAVE A FULFILLED
AND HAPPY LIFE.

If you would like to share your story on how this book helped you, or offer any comments, I would love to hear from you. Please contact me at: arsen@thedontdiebook.com